TALES FROM THE
CHICAGO BLACKHAWKS
LOCKER ROOM

A COLLECTION OF THE GREATEST
BLACKHAWKS STORIES EVER TOLD

HARVEY WITTENBERG
FOREWORD BY BRUCE WOLF

SPORTS
PUBLISHING

Sports Publishing books may be purchased in bulk at special discounts for sales promotion, corporate gifts, fund-raising, or educational purposes. Special editions can also be created to specifications. For details, contact the Special Sales Department, Sports Publishing, 307 West 36th Street, 11th Floor, New York, NY 10018 or sportspubbooks@skyhorsepublishing.com.

Sports Publishing® is a registered trademark of Skyhorse Publishing, Inc.®, a Delaware corporation.

Visit our website at www.sportspubbooks.com

10 9 8 7 6 5 4 3 2 1

Library of Congress Cataloging-in-Publication Data is available on file.

ISBN: 978-1-61321-082-6

Printed in the United States of America

This book is dedicated to my loving daughters, Sue, Elizabeth, Melissa, and Michelle plus my grandchildren, Julia, Ryan, and Jeremy, the memory of my father, Irving, who took me to my first Blackhawk game when I was only ten and hockey fans everywhere!

In addition, to the memory of Blackhawk players who helped make this original book possible who have passed: Keith Magnuson, Pit Martin, Reg Fleming, and Bob Probert. Also to the memory of owner Bill Wirtz, coach Billy Reay, and general manager Tommy Ivan.

FOREWORD

In the waning days of the old Chicago Stadium, someone came up with a slogan to resurrect the fans' delirium in that most intimate arena: "Remember the roar!" Me, I remember a solitary voice, Harvey Wittenberg's "One minute to play in the period." What a lovely drone. So far removed from many of today's cheerleading, self-infatuated public address announcers. Harvey Wittenberg did not need to stir the Stadium crowd, already on edge over the world's fastest sport. "One minute to play in the period" was a stoic counterpoint to the thunder of that mammoth stadium organ, itself an echo of the 16,666 fans' din. In the chaos of the scramble for a tying or winning goal, the stern voice of time running out would intone: "One minute to play in the period." No betrayal of emotion permitted. Judgment hour was at hand. Not that Harvey Wittenberg wouldn't indulge in an uptilt at other times. "Blackhawk goal, scored by number 9, Bobby Hull," had Harvey lingering on "Hull," almost creating a five hole between the last two "Ls" of "Hull."

There are so many sounds of the Chicago Stadium that grip the mind's ear. The hollow pop of empty beer cups crushed after the game. The jingle to Tab cola being hammered out on that most ornate organ by the nine-fingered Al Melgard (like "Nike" being swooshed onto the ceiling of the Sistine Chapel by Michelangelo?) The jeering from the crowd at a certain referee: "Ashley's a bum, Ashley's a bum, Ashley's a bum!" Remember when jeering was so innocent? And Harvey Wittenberg saying, "The Stadium will pay a 100 dollar reward to anyone who can immediately identify anyone throwing any debris on the ice that will lead to their arrest and conviction." Even that had magic to it. Because it was all part of the Blackhawks. Of Bobby, Stan and Tony O. Of Thanksgiving night, 1968, when Jim Pappin took a slap shot that was deflected into the club circle seats behind the goal, and I tried to barehand the puck and was lucky my thumb wasn't torn off. Of April 5, 1970, when through some questionable means my father got me a mezzanine seat, and I watched the Montreal Canadiens pull their goalie in the third period for an extra man because they need to score a certain number of goals to make the playoffs. And the Hawks scored five empty net goals to win 10-2. And through it all, Harvey's is the constant voice. Like a reassuring Gregorian chant, "Blackhawk goal scored by number 18, Denis Savard, assisted by number 20, Al Secord and number 28, Steve Larmer at 19:59." A voice etched into our hearts as much as that Indian head emblem. I have only one more wish, now that the Blackhawks have won a Stanley Cup in 2010 is that they bring Harvey back for the next Cup that he makes one more announcement: "Remember there is no smoking in the United Center, and by the way, ladies and gentlemen, here is the Stanely Cup!"

—Bruce Wolf

PREFACE

It's been more than 65 years since I saw my first Blackhawk game at the Chicago Stadium in a classic Stanely Cup battle against Montreal. While I enjoy all sports, for me hockey is number one. I feel it is the best sport as a professional to announce or report on and as a spectator to watch. I have been lucky to have the opportunity to work in a field and sport that I enjoy for more than 50 years to be involved with the Chicago Blackhawks. I am currently reporting on the Blackhawk web page with history, features, and a column plus handling the press box announcing for the media at the United Center while occasionally doing the public address announcing as a backup. The enjoyment of writing this book by reconnecting with the many players, coaches and others from the Hawk past plus interviewing the new young Hawks from 2010 Cup team. These tales brought back a number of stories of players and coaches who are no longer with us. I found some new information that hadn't been told before plus the fun of seeing a lot of the Hawk alumni returning to meet the fans at the United Center and at Fan Conventions. I hope you enjoy these stories and that I have an opportunity to tell a lot more in the future. Enjoy!

—Harvey Wittenberg

ACKNOWLEDGMENTS

Special thanks to Rocky Wirtz, John McDonough, Jay Blunt, Stan Bowman, Pete Hassen, Brandon Faber, Adam Rogowin, Bill Smith, and the Chicago Blackhawks' public relations staff.

INTRODUCTION

Blackhawk dreams came through in Philadelphia on June 9, 2010 in Game 6 of the Stanley Cup finals with Chicago's 4-3 win in overtime on Patrick Kane's goal even though we were still waiting for the red goal lamp to go on! The team's fourth Stanely Cup ended a 49 year absence and while it came on the road as it did in 1961, millions of Chicagoans turned out on June 11, 2010 to salute the city's newest champions! Blackhawk fans have been blessed with great players and records ever since they played their first National Hockey League game on November 17, 1926, a 4-1 victory over the Toronto St. Pats. The current resurgence of the Hawks through the leadership of Rocky Wirtz and John McDonough has not only brought a Stanely Cup, but the return of favorites and Hall of Famers Stan Mikita, Bobby Hull, Denis Savard, and Tony Esposito as team ambassadors. NHL records like three goals in only 21 seonds and 503 straight starts by a goalie without wearing a protective mask are two Blackhawk records that may never be broken! Billy Mosienko tallied the fastest three goals by a single player on the last day of the regular season on March 23, 1952 in New York against the Rangers in a 7-6 win. Glenn Hall started 503 consecutive games in goal, all maskless from October 6, 1955 to November 7, 1962. There's no doubt that the salary cap has made things difficult for teams to repeat as champions, but the Hawks have made some wise moves in locking up core players and building good draft picks to have a solid future. Winning the cup with team average age of 27.4 which was only up from 25.5 in 2009 shows what can be done. I hope you enjoy the addition of tales from the new Hawk players and adding some old ones that are interesting and hopefully amusing. "GO HAWKS!"

BLACKHAWK TALES

Blackhawk Landscape Changes

The fate of the Chicago franchise changed dramatically in 1952 when James Norris and Arthur Wirtz purchased the floundering team, which had finished out of the playoffs for six straight seasons. Then came the hiring of Tommy Ivan as general manager away from the successful Detroit Red Wings in July, 1954. Ivan had coached the Wings to six straight first-place finishes and three Stanley Cups.

Although he never played in the NHL because of his size, he was an excellent judge of talent and a tough negotiator when players wanted more money. Ivan was the great Gordie Howe's first pro coach in 1945 at Omaha and then for seven years at Detroit.

Arthur Wirtz with Tony Esposito

The Hawks were in bad shape when Ivan arrived, making the playoffs only once in seven seasons, and he was not able to get them back into postseason play in his first four campaigns. Ivan therefore fired head coach Sid Abel who played for him in Detroit before finishing his career in Chicago.

Coaching Shuffle

Ivan then brought in Buffalo minor league coach Frank Eddolls, who lasted one season. Following that short stint, Ivan brought back the legendary Dick Irvin, who played for the team in their first two years in the NHL (1926-29). Irvin coached the Hawks in 1930-31 before being fired. (Irvin went on to win four Stanley Cup championships: one with Toronto and three with Montreal.) In the meantime Ivan put himself in the hot seat for a season and a half before bringing on Rudy Pilous who coached Chicago's junior team, St. Catharine's. Pilous guided the team to its most recent Stanley Cup (1961) and lasted two more years beyond that before being replaced by Billy Reay (1963-1977) who is Chicago's winningest coach with 516 wins—more than the Hawks' following three coaches combined.

Hawks' Collegiate Flavor Starts Trend

Chicago lost one of it's all-time fan favorites—Keith Magnuson (Maggie)—in a tragic car crash in December 2003 at the age of 56. The President of the Blackhawk Alumni Association was coming back from attending a funeral for a former player. It is fitting that Keith's #3 jersey was retired along with Hall of Famer Pierre Pilote on November 12, 2008. While Keith's name is not listed in the team's record books, his hard work and dedication earned him a spot on the Hawk's 75th Anniversary Squad by fan vote in 2000. The popular defenseman never played in the minors, came out of Denver University as a player, then assistant coach, and head Hawk coach for one and a half seasons. Chicago was perhaps the first NHL team to have four U.S. college players in its lineup in 1969-70 with Keith and Denver U teammates liff Koroll and Jim Wiste along with goalie Tony Esposito (Michigan Tech).

Tough Negotiations

Maggie was eager to sign with Chicago, but relied on his assistant coach in college, Harry Ottenbreit, to act as his agent. They met Hawk GM Ivan at the Brown Palace Hotel, and Ottenbreit told Maggie not to talk. Harry told Ivan that Maggie wanted a $100,000 signing bonus and a five-year deal for $100,000 per season—both of which were unheard of in 1969. Ivan informed them that the negotiations were over, and when Maggie tried to speak, Harry grabbed his leg under the table. When all was said and done, Ivan gave Magnuson a $500 bonus and a $15,000 contract, which incidentally is what Gordie Howe got his first year with Detroit 24 years earlier when Ivan coached him. Maggie told me that little did Ivan know that he would have gladly played for nothing.

Roaring Stadium

Maggie had never been to the old Chicago Stadium, and Ottenbreit warned him that he was in for a surprise. When Keith played his first game there, he told me that the feeling

Keith Magnuson

was unbelievable when he climbed the stairs from the locker room to the ice to hear the roar of the crowd.

Veteran Coach Reay was starting his seventh season with Chicago and wasn't delighted about having a rookie defenseman like Maggie in his lineup following a year where the Hawks finished last in the East (1968-69). Maggie was not blessed with the greatest skills, but always gave 100 percent every time he took to the ice. On his first shift in his first preseason game, which came against Montreal, he knocked Canadien tough guy, John Ferguson, into the bench! Maggie went on to 213 penalty minutes in his rookie season, which was a team record at the time, and recorded 1,442 minutes in the penalty box in 11 seasons. That was also a Chicago career mark until it was eclipsed by Chris Chelios (1,495 penalty minutes from 1991-99).

Goal Scoring by Hull, Not Magnuson

Maggie's rookie season was indeed a memorable one, on and off the ice. Not only did the Hawks become the first NHL team to go from last place to first in a season, Esposito set a modern-day record of 15 shutouts to earn the rookie of the year honors, and Bobby Hull became the third player in history to score 500 career goals. It also saw Hull hold out for a new contract for the first 15 games, and the surprise retirement of winger Kenny Wharram due to a heart condition during training camp.

The Hawks lost their first five games before a 1-1 tie in New York with Maggie's college teammate, Cliff Koroll, getting his first NHL goal. In the next game in Montreal, Esposito registered his first of 74 shutouts as a Blackhawk against the team that gave him up.

Never known as a prolific scorer, Maggie had only 14 goals in his NHL career; in fact, his highest season total was three in 1970-71. He was involved in one of the strangest games ever at the Chicago Stadium in his first season. It was April 5, 1970 against Montreal. The Hawks needed a victory to finish first ahead of Boston in the final game of the season, and the Canadiens needed a win, tie or to score more goals to move past the New York Rangers to get into the playoffs. After an initial Canadien goal, the Hawks took command and built up a 5-2 lead early in the third period. The desperate Canadiens pulled their goalie for an extra attacker for more than 12 minutes in hopes of scoring three more goals to get into the playoffs, which they hadn't missed in 22 seasons. Maggie had 24 assists, but no goals in his first season, so when the net became empty, his teammates kept trying to feed him to no avail!

Chicago got five empty-net goals to make the final 10-2 and go from last to first, passing up Boston. However, after the Hawks swept Detroit in the first round of the playoffs, Boston gained revenge by doing the same to the Hawks behind the play of all-star Bobby Orr on their way to the Stanley Cup over St. Louis.

Rookie Pranks and More

Veterans took pleasure in having good-natured fun with rookies like Maggie. Defenseman Pat Stapleton and Stan Mikita took Maggie and another rookie, Terry Caffery, out to a field in Elmhurst for a "snipe hunt." They gave them the necessary equipment, a potato sack and a flashlight plus the instructions—just call, "snipe, snipe" and if that doesn't work start whistling. Maggie and Caffery did what they were told when a police car showed up and the police asked what they were doing. Maggie replied, "snipe hunting." The officer asked, "Where's your license?" Maggie and Caffery replied, "We don't have one!" The police took them to the station and in a darkened courtroom, the judge pronounced his sentence: "30 days, no bond," and they were taken to a jail cell. Two hours later, Mikita and Stapleton showed up and took them to the players' favorite watering hole for a good laugh. Welcome to the Blackhawks!

Maggie Observes History!

Maggie will never forget February 21, 1970 at the Stadium against the Rangers. Hull became the third player in history to score 500 career goals when his patented slap shot whistled past goalie Ed Giacomin as the crowd noise exploded and the ice was littered with thousands of hats. I know it took me a few minutes to announce the historic goal over the roar. Maggie said he never heard anything like it.

Superstition

A lot of athletes and coaches are somewhat superstitious. Billy Reay always wore a hat behind the Hawk bench. Maggie and his roommate, Cliff Koroll, were no different. Their first year saw several long unbeaten strings, so when driving to the stadium, they were determined to do the same thing as long as the streak was intact. This meant driving non-stop from the western suburbs to the stadium without applying the brakes —even while going through red lights. Fortunately, they had no accidents.

Boxing Lessons

Maggie always took a lot of kidding about his many on-ice fights, especially when it was learned that he took boxing lessons from former Chicago boxing champion, Johnny Coulon, at his west side gym on Division Street. In a preseason game in Toronto, Maggie won his first fight against Mike Walton, which apparently convinced GM Ivan to sign the feisty redhead to a contract.

One of Maggie's more memorable tussles came against the great Bobby Orr, who later became a teammate at the end of his all-too-brief NHL career. Maggie had gotten under Orr's skin during a game at the Boston Garden, and with less than a minute left in the game, Orr went after the Hawk rookie, which wound up in a draw. Maggie never backed down from a fight and was usually booed by fans when the Hawks played on the road. However, Maggie never tried to provoke veteran stars like Gordie Howe and John Ferguson. His biggest fighting rival was probably Philadelphia's Dave Schultz. Maggie said Schultz was the toughest guy he fought and that the burly Flyer who still holds the NHL record for penalty minutes in a season (472) probably got the best of him in the dozen or so fights.

Blackhawk Alumni

Maggie remained president of the Blackhawk Alumni until his untimely death and has been replaced by teammate and friend Cliff Koroll. Maggie told me that he was very fortunate to be in Chicago at a time with great players like Mikita, Hull, Esposito, Savard, Doug Wilson, Bill White, and briefly Bobby Orr to mention a few plus coaches like Bill Reay and Bob Pulford along with GM Tommy Ivan.

Coaches Don't Outlast Players

Regarding his brief stint as Hawks' Coach, Maggie said Ivan told him, "Coaches are hired to be fired," and Al Arbour, who coached the New York Islanders to four straight Cups, said "You aren't good until you're fired twice." Maggie told me that he feels a lot of today's players are missing passion and intensity and that successful teams need at least six leaders. Also, Bobby Hull told him that the third period separates the men from the boys. Maggie knew that Chicago was a great city with terrific fans. "It takes a long time to build a winner and you only get certain runs, but harmony and the challenge to work together will be the key to a great future for the Blackhawks." Maggie always displayed the pride of the Indian head until he died.

Hawk Jersey No. 3 Retired!

November 12, 2008 saw the jerseys of Pierre Pilote and Magnuson officially retired. Pilote's eight straight All-Star selections and three straight Norris Trophies as the league's top defenseman were just some of the credentials for this Hall of Famer who toiled 13 seasons for the Hawks, seven as team captain—a record that might be eclipsed by Jonathan Toews. Pilote's career was highly praised by other league All-Stars like Orr, Denis Potvin, and Montreal's Larry Robinson.

Pilote Leads Team in Stanley Cup Points

On the '61 Stanley Cup championship team, Pierre led the team in total points during the playoffs, which was great for a defenseman playing with the likes of Mikita and Hull. Pilote still ranks second among Chicago blue liners in assists with 400, second to Doug Wilson.

Somewhat copying some of the offensive moves that were partially started by Montreal's Doug Harvey, Pilote added more of his own offensive style with puck possession, skating and crisp passing as opposed to what most defensemen were accustomed to doing in the '40s and '50s which was known as "dump and chase" the puck. Pilote said he emulated the offensive moves of one of his favorite players—New York center Edgar Laprade.

Pete's Speed and Passing Are Excellent!

Pilote's skating ability enabled him to lead rushes and get passes to Mikita, Hull and Wharram. Pete's up-tempo play encouraged the next super-star defenseman—Bobby Orr—to carry Boston's offense for 10 years.

Pete, said, "It helped to play the way I did when you had a great goalie behind you like Glenn Hall and my partners like Elmer "Moose" Vasko and Doug Jarrett who stayed back when I was racing up the ice. Also, it was easier to get passes to speedy wingers like Wharram, Mikita and Hull."

Howie Young: The Wild One

Pete remembers the controversial Howie Young who before joining Chicago was known as Detroit's "bad boy" for his many run-ins by trying to stop Bobby Hull. While in Toronto to face the Maple Leafs, Pilote got a call from a country music bar that a drunk Young fell down the stairs. Being the captain, and facing an 11 p.m. curfew plus an early skate the next day at10 a.m., Pete went to get Young and bring him back to the Royal York Hotel. Young was rooming with Bill Hay, and Pilote got him back in time. The next morning at

Bobby Orr

practice, Young was clearly hung over and could barely skate. Pete told Hay that he brought Howie back, but Hay said that afterwards Young had staggered out again and returned to the room at 5 a.m.

Young, Fleming and Eddie Shack

Another time in Chicago against Toronto, the Leafs' Eddie Shack belted Young over the boards early in the game. Later in the period, Shack got the puck behind his net and picked up speed as he moved up ice with his head down. Reggie Fleming saw an opportunity to even matters. He caught Shack with a check that flipped him in the air, which earned Reggie a major penalty. The Stadium crowd went crazy as Young jumped on the ice and hoisted Reggie on his shoulders and skated around before Reggie got to the penalty box. Although Reggie was never a big scorer in his four years with the Hawks —21 goals to be exact—his biggest shot came in Game 6 of the Stanley Cup finals in Detroit. His short-hander tied the score as Chicago went on to whip the Red Wings 5-1 to win the cup in '61.

Pilote's Rookie Season

Most players can clearly recall their rookie season, and Pilote is no exception. When he was called up in '55-56, he played 20 games with veteran coach Dick Irvin in charge. Before a game in Toronto, Frank Martin was nursing a sore back, and the trainer had wrapped a sponge around him. Irvin came in and saw it and said, "Hey Mar-tan, unless you take that mattress off your back, you ain't playing!" It was Pierre's first game after being called up from Buffalo, and his parents wanted to drive up from Fort Erie to see him play, but Pierre told them that being his first game, he wouldn't see much action and talked them out of it. Much to his surprise, when he got to Maple Leaf Garden, Irvin put him in the starting line-up. On the opening faceoff, Tod Sloan broke in over the blue line and slipped the puck between the rookie's legs. Pierre recalls that Hawk goalie Hank Bassen made the big save; otherwise he could have been benched the rest of the game. He didn't make another mistake and went on to play nearly half the game thanks to the "mattress" on Martin's back.

Pilote Recalls Veteran Coach Dick Irvin

Irvin coached 1,449 games in the NHL with 692 wins, which ranks him as the third-winningest coach of all time behind Scotty Bowman and Al Arbour. Pierre said he was always very nosy.

Following a game in New York, the team was due to take a long train ride back to Chicago. The locker room was small, so the players had to store their luggage in another room. Veteran Allan Stanley who spent 21 seasons in the NHL with five different teams, including Chicago, filled his suitcase up with beer, which made it very heavy. The nosy Irvin checked the bags, and in his cynical tone said, "Stanley, your suitcase better weigh the same when you get off the train!"

Pete Earns Respect
Without a Fight

Pierre was never known as a fighter, although he never backed away from a fight as he compiled 1,206 penalty minutes in 13 seasons. In a game against Montreal, he did earn the respect of one of the toughest forwards of the time, John Ferguson, whom he had several tilts with in the American Hockey League (AHL). Ferguson was moving in with his head down and Pierre could have leveled him, but instead just poked the puck away, and Fergie realized that he caught a break. That "free pass" from Pilote earned Fergie's respect and the pair never battled.

Glasses and Al Arbour

Al Arbour, who won four Stanley Cups with the Islanders and is second in all-time wins as a coach, was one of the few players to ever wear glasses in the NHL. Al played 16 seasons in the NHL with four teams including three years in Chicago. Pierre said Al tried to play without glasses, but during a preseason game he went into the corner for the puck and started skating out without it. Pierre yelled to him that he didn't have the puck, and instead he was stick handling with a piece of a stick that had black tape on it. After that, Al kept his glasses on, and it didn't stop him from diving or attempting to block shots.

Louie, Louie Plus Al

Popular Lou Angotti, who assisted on many big goals scored by Bobby Hull, roomed with Al MacNeil, who joined the Hawks for four seasons in 1962. Later, it was MacNeil who was head coach at Montreal in 1971 when they dealt Chicago a heartbreaking defeat in Game 7 for the Stanley Cup. Lou and Al maintained their friendship for years with an exchange of letters. One of the last ones came from the dry-humored MacNeil, who wrote simply, "I have nothing to say! Regards, Al."

"Crash" Breaks Mohns's Jaw

Defenseman Ian "Crash" Cushenan had a brief two-season stay in Chicago ('56-'58). Pilote recalled a game in Boston when Doug Mohns, who later joined the Hawks as part of the scooter line with Mikita and Kenny Wharram, was with the Bruins. Mohns knocked the stick out of Crash's hands, and twice pushed it away from him when the Hawk tried to pick it up. However, on the third time, Crash belted Mohns, breaking his jaw.

Moose

Pilote's playing partner for 10 years was Elmer "Moose" Vasko, who was the biggest player in the NHL at some 230 pounds. And while Pete was moving up on rushes, the slower

Vasko hung back. Moose did not have a high pain threshold. In New York, he hurt his ankle, and the doctor gave him a cortizone shot and told him he would be fine, and to just drink a few beers. It wasn't until Moose got back to Chicago that it was discovered that he had a broken ankle.

Pete Played with Three All-Time Hawk Greats

Pilote feels fortunate that he played with three of the greatest Hawks and NHL players of all-time: Hull, Mikita and Hall. All three have their jerseys hanging from the United Center rafters. "I feel Hall was the best goalie I ever saw or played with. Some say Sawchuk was better, but that was probably because when he was in Detroit, he had a stronger team in front of him.

"Stan was the greatest pound for pound. He was durable, tough, crafty, set up his linemates, and could score, besides playing both penalty-killing and on the power play.

"For the fans, Bobby was the greatest. When he wound up behind the net and started skating with guys hanging all over him then firing a puck at some 100-plus miles per hour, it always brought the crowd to their feet."

Although his play was not as flashy as Hull, Mikita and Hall, eight-straight All-Star selections and three consecutive Norris Trophies in a six-team league merit more than enough consideration in having Pilote's number 3 jersey retired. Although it's been more than 35 years since Pierre skated for

Chicago, and many recent fans have never seen him play, time should not bypass his accomplishments, because Pete Pilote was too good to be overlooked!

Low Salaries

Hockey salaries in the '40s, '50s, '60s and leading up to start of the World Hockey Association in the early '70s were meager to say the least. You were lucky to earn double digits unless you were a big star. The dollar exchange rate between the U.S. and Canada was close, unlike today. Reggie Fleming told me his last contract in the '60s was $9,500 plus incentives that he never reached.

Stan Mitka: A Sports Agent?

Hawk GM Tommy Ivan was a tough negotiator, so when first-round draft pick JP Bordeleau was offered his first contract in 1970, he needed some advice. On a plane ride back from a preseason game in Montreal, Ivan asked Bordeleau to sign the agreement. The young French-Canadian didn't have an agent, and "Arliss Michaels" hadn't been invented yet, nor had *Jerry McGuire* even been scripted! Bordeleau went to the back of the plane to show it to veteran Stan Mikita. The Hawk All-Star center read it over, declined an agent fee, and told Bordeleau to sign it: "It's a good deal!" JP did and went back to Mr. Ivan to give him the contract.

Splitting the Red Sea and Blue Line

Bordeleau played 10 years with the Hawks from 1970-1980 and wound up with 97 goals and 223 assists in 519 games. He told me about his first two-goal game back in January '73 at the Stadium against the Boston Bruins. The Hawks were trailing 4-3 when JP scored to tie the game going into the third period. He took a pass in center ice and raced into the Bruin zone. Then JP made a quick head fake that caused both Boston defenders to split in opposite directions, leaving the middle wide open, and he scored to give the Hawks a 5-4 win. After the game, talking to the media, JP was asked what happened on the winning goal. The modest JP said, "It was like the parting of the Red Sea!" Strong words from a young hockey player. The next day at practice, JP was one of the last guys to get on the ice. When the new hero stepped out, his teammates formed two lines and bowed down chanting, "Moses, Moses!"

Million-Dollar Line

The late Murray Balfour joined the Hawks in 1959 for five seasons and became the right wing on the famed "million-dollar baby line" with Bobby Hull and Bill Hay. Balfour scored a key goal in the third overtime against Montreal in the '61 semifinals at the Stadium as the Hawks went on to their third Stanley Cup.

While living in Chicago, Balfour roomed with Reggie

Fleming. Balfour was a bachelor and liked to play poker a lot. Reggie told me that Balfour made so much money playing poker that he never cashed his team paycheck that season and also took his poker-playing buddies to Las Vegas at his expense. Also, Balfour was lazy about parking his car in the northside neighborhood and usually parked in front of a fire hydrant. Reggie asked him at the end of the season how many tickets he received with his Ontario license plates. Murray replied, "Only 52."

Expense Accounts

One of the unsung heroes of the Hawks is the security guard at the Blackhawk dressing room, John Robertson who along with his late father, has prevented unwanted visitors from trying to gain access to the players since the late 1930s. In those early days, not only were the salaries low, but the expense accounts for meals, cabs and buses were even smaller. Bill Tobin was the general manager then, and always had a watchful eye on costs. Defenseman Alex Levinsky, who played five seasons (1934-39) on the first two Stanley Cup teams, used to try to brown bag his meals on the road to collect expenses. Robertson recalls that when Tobin recruited the late Harold "Mush" March, he pulled out a wad of bills and gave Mush $15 to join the team in 1928! March paid off by scoring the winning goal in the second overtime for Chicago's first Stanley Cup in 1934. March played for 17 seasons until 1945 and then became a linesman. He was the first linesman to wear glasses. Mush often worked the lines at the Stadium with George Hayes, who quit when the NHL asked him to take an eye test.

Billy Mosienko

Billy Mosienko, who holds the record for the fastest three goals (21 seconds) by an individual, had a brilliant 14-year career with the Hawks, scoring 258 goals. He was part of the famed, but too brief Chicago pony line with Doug and Max Bentley. In the '40s the game was a lot more physical, and players seemed to play even when hurt. Mosienko hurt his leg and in order to fool his opponents, he had the trainer put a bandage pad on his good leg! I remember when Mosienko came back to the Chicago Stadium to play in an alumni game during the preseason against St. Louis alumni. It was more than 30 years after he retired from the Hawks in 1955. The two-time all-star still had a hop in his step and he scored in that game. It reminded me of the way he played in his prime, outskating defensemen and sweeping in to score.

Mike O'Connell: First Chicago-Born Player to Play for the Hawks

Mike O'Connell was a third round pick in 1975 from the Kingston Junior team, and became the first Chicago native to skate for the Hawks in 1978. He played for parts of four seasons in his hometown and nine more campaigns in the NHL with Detroit and Boston. He later became GM for the Boston Bruins. While in Chicago, the Hakws finished first in the Smythe Division his first three seasons and second the season he was traded. Mike told me after going to Chicago Stadium in his youth, it was even more exciting during the '70s when the team was dominating its division. He also said as a rookie in the locker room, he thought it was odd that a lot of players had ashtrays in their stalls and during training camp, there were cots for the players to rest on during the rigorous two-a-day workout sessions.

Chicago-Area Hawks

There have been several other Chicago area natives who have played for the Hawks. The most famous are Eddie Olczyk and Chris Chelios. Eddie is currently handling color of Hawk TV sportscasts and also nationally and Chelios finally retired in 2010 at age 48. Others include goalies Craig Anderson and Bob Janeczyk and winger Mark LaVarre. There may be more on the way since the Hawks have several draftees in their system.

Eddie Olczyk

The toughest debut for a hometown player probably belongs to Olczyk. The pressure of being a No. 1 draft pick and third overall was a lot in 1984. Eddie started and ended his career with the Hawks, but in between he was with five other teams over 16 seasons and scored 324 goals in his career.

Behn Wilson: Sleeping Giant

In the '84-85 season, GM Bob Pulford fired Orval Tessier and took over as coach with 27 games left on the schedule. Pully ran practices a lot different than Orval. In the first practice, Pully ran what is called a containment drill. Eddie tried to make an impression against veteran defenseman Behn Wilson who was moving up ice. Eddie took the puck away from Behn

Eddie Olczyk

and went up ice to score. After practice, the towering Behn cornered Eddie and told him, "Never take the puck away from me, even in practice." Eddie realized rookies are to be seen, not heard. However, after that, Behn turned out to be a protector for Eddie. Two weeks later against Detroit, veteran Dwight Foster gave Eddie a knee and Behn came across the ice and grabbed Foster. Behn told Foster if he ever hit Eddie again, he would get it from him.

Phil Esposito: Starts with Hawks...
Becomes All-Star in Boston

After the famed "million-dollar line" of Bobby Hull, Bill Hay and Murray Balfour was broken up in 1964, coach Billy Reay teamed up Hull with Phil Esposito and Chico Maki. Esposito had been playing for the Hawks' farm team in St. Louis and was brought up in the 1963-64 campaign when he appeared in 27 games. After four seasons, Esposito was traded to Boston and later the Rangers. With the Hawks he scored 74 goals, but after the trade, he broke an NHL record with 76 goals in 1970-71. He wound up his 16-season career with 717 goals to rank among the top 10 in league history.

Phil Meets His Hockey Idol,
Gordie Howe, Head On

Phil had a funloving air about him, but that didn't always sit well with Coach Reay or GM Tommy Ivan. He remembers his second NHL game against Detroit. He hadn't seen much ice time, and his feet were killing him, so he untied his skates with just a few minutes left to play in the game. Coach Reay told him to go in. Phil quickly tied his laces and went on the ice with Bobby Hull. He looked up and was facing Red Wing greats Gordie Howe, Ted Lindsay and Alex Delvecchio. Bobby

Phil Esposito

yelled, "Look out for that old number 9 (Howe)." Phil looked up at Howe, who blinked with a smile on his lips. Then the puck was dropped and Howe knocked the rookie in the mouth with an elbow. Phil fell back and said, "You old S.O.B!" as he speared his one-time hockey idol. The referee sent both of them to the penalty box. In those days at the Detriot Olympia, a policeman usually sat in the middle to keep the players separated. Phil applied a towel to his bloody lip, glared at Howe as he leaned across the guard and said, "You used to be my idol." The veteran Howe glared back and said, "What did you say, rookie?" Sheepishly, Phil replied, "Nothing, Mr. Howe!" When Phil got back to the dressing room, Hull advised him that Gordie always tests rookies.

A Bobby Hull Tattoo?

Phil, Bobby and Chico would always work out certain plays. One night in Chicago, Phil was taking the faceoff in the attack zone. He told Bobby he would get the puck back to him and then drive to the net. That's the way it went, and Bobby blasted his slap shot, but the 100-mile-per-hour missile struck Esposito flat in his rear. Fortunately it happened late in the game, and Phil was in extreme pain. When taking his shower after the game, the trainer told Phil that the Blackhawk imprint from the puck was on his butt.

Wise Guy

Phil's funloving nature off the ice always seemed to get him in trouble with Coach Reay, although on the ice he managed three straight seasons of 20-plus goals before being traded to Boston. In his first season, he usually didn't get much ice time, and in February '64 at Maple Leaf Garden, he hadn't played at all. There was about a minute left and the Hawks were down three goals when Coach Reay tapped him on the shoulder to send him into the game. Phil turned around and said, "Do you want me to win it or tie it?" After Phil made the remark, Reay said, "Sit down!"

One Hundred Bottles of Beer Against the Wall

In Detroit, after celebrating a victory, Phil and linemates Hull and Maki were enjoying a few beers in their hotel room. Knowing that the coach was on a different floor, they started throwing bottles against the wall. The next morning, Phil found out that the coach gave up his suite to a newlywed couple and in fact was in the room next door to the beer party.

Phone Calls Interrupt Contract Talks?

Phil also had his run-ins with GM Tommy Ivan when it came to contract talks. He went into Tommy's office with the hopes of getting a raise—to $8,000—after his first 20-plus goal season. As the talks started, the phone rang and Tommy got into an animated conversation and told the caller, "I'll never pay you that!" and hung up. Getting back to Phil, Tommy said, "Now what did you say you wanted?" Phil said, "I feel I deserve at least $8,000." Again, the phone rang, and Tommy got in another heated "conversation." Then Tommy said to Phil, "How much did you say?" Phil replied, "$7,500 will be fine Mr. Ivan." Years later, Phil asked Tommy if he had a button under his desk to make his phone ring, and the wily GM said, "I'll never tell!"

Behind the Green Door

There was a place behind the Mount Royal Hotel that the players called the "Green Door," where they replenished their thirst after a hard-fought tie game. Phil, Hull, Maki, Mikita, Kenny Wharram, Doug Mohns and Pat Stapleton were there downing a few quarts while I was nursing my sole bottle. There was another guy at the end of the table between Esposito and Mikita whom I didn't know. A few weeks later, an article that wasn't too complimentary came out about the Hawks. It turned out the guy was a writer for *Sports Illustrated*. Right after the article came out at the next game, Phil pulled me aside and thought I knew that guy at the "Green Door" in Montreal was a reporter. I told him I thought he was a friend of his or Mikita.

Missed a Chance to Play with Tony

Phil was named to the Hockey Hall of Fame in 1984 and recalled to me that he had hoped to finish his career with the Blackhawks and play with his brother Tony. A trade was set in 1978 to send him from the Rangers to Chicago for Jim Harrison, but at the last minute, the New York owner nixed the deal.

Helps to Bring Savard Back

Phil still regards the Blackhawk jersey as the best in the NHL and did the Hawks a favor when he was GM of Tampa Bay. At trade deadline Chicago asked if Denis Savard would be available. Esposito called Denis and asked him if he wanted to go back to the Hawks to finish his great career. Savy returned to play the last 12 regular-season games in 1995 and led the Hawks in playoff scoring as they advanced to the conference finals. Denis went on to play two more seasons before retiring in June 1997.

Mikita: An Extra Coach

In 1978, the Hawks' No. 1 draft pick was Tim Higgins. In that same draft, the 10th-round pick was Darryl Sutter. Higgins played six years with the Hawks before finishing his career with New Jersey and Detroit. Higgy broke in in '78 and was an eager rookie but did not get a lot of ice time. Outside of stoppage in play, coaches usually call a player's name or tap him on the shoulder to go into the game. The Hawks were trailing and were killing a penalty against Detroit when Higgy got the tap and jumped on the ice, which immediately resulted in too many men on the ice, putting his team down two players. The coach yelled at him, "What are you doing?" Tim turned back to the bench and saw Mikita smiling and realized where the tap on his shoulder came from.

First College Player on the Hawks: Billy Hay

William "Don't call me Red" Hay was the first U.S. college grad to play for the Hawks. In his rookie season (1959-60), he won NHL rookie honors—the Calder Trophy—and ranked second on the team in points (18-37=55). He centered what

became Chicago's "million-dollar line" by accident. Injuries around Christmas time to Eric Nesterenko and Ron Murphy forced coach Rudy Pilous to shuffle Bobby Hull with Hay and Murray Balfour. The trio combined for 75 goals, with Hull leading the team with 39. That trio combined for 260 goals in

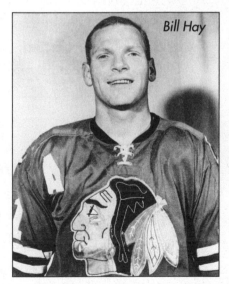

Bill Hay

the next four seasons with the Stanley Cup coming in Hay's second season ('61).

Hay graduated from Colorado College and played eight seasons. He had retired in 1966, but at the urging of GM Tommy Ivan, came back in January, 1967 for the last 36 games to help Chicago to its first first-place finish in NHL team history. Hay currently serves as chairman and chief executive officer of the Hockey Hall of Fame.

Rainbow Arena and Quick Practices

The Hawks used to practice at Rainbow Arena on Chicago's north side, which was demolished in 2003. Coach Pilous had an easy going demeanor, and although Hay was not a prankster, he did manage to fool the coach a few times. The team usually practiced for about 90 minutes. The clock at the rink was just above the players' bench, and it didn't have any protection. When Pilous turned his back to run some drills, the tall Hay pushed the clock ahead 10 minutes. He did it several times in between his turns on the ice, and the practice ran about a half hour instead of the usual time, and the coach never caught on.

Economy Transportation

Being a college graduate, newly married and playing when salaries weren't more than $7,500, Hay drove an economy car that was pretty banged up. Driving to a game at the Stadium, Hay let veteran Ted Lindsay drive along with Glen Skov and

Eric Nesterenko. In Chicago, Lindsay drove through a red light and was stopped by the police. The officer told Lindsay he would have to take them to the police station. Lindsay said, "I'm Ted Lindsay, and we play for the Blackhawks and we are on our way to play tonight." The policeman replied, "Lindsay would never drive a wreck like this." Hay, sitting in the back seat, said, "Officer, can you let us go before you insult my car any more?" To show their appreciation, they gave the officer a couple of tickets to the game. They made it to the stadium on time and won the game.

"Red" a No-No!

All the sports writers covering the Hawks always referred to Hay as "Red," and even my predecessor announced his name as "Red." When I took over as stadium public address announcer in December, 1961 and introduced myself to number 11, he told me, "My name is Bill, don't announce my name as 'Red.'"

Eric Nesterenko: Movie Star?

Some may recall the 1986 movie *Youngblood* starring Rob Lowe and Patrick Swayze as hockey players, with former Hawk Eric Nesterenko as Lowe's father. But Eric had a much longer career in hockey. The right-winger played 16 seasons with the Hawks from 1956 to 1972 and ranks third on the team in games played (1,013) behind Mikita and Hull. He is 14th in points, 15th in assists, and 17th in goals.

College Star: Chicago's Part-Time Hockey Player

Nesterenko had great scoring statistics with the Toronto Marlies junior team and was compared to Montreal's Jean Beliveau. Eric never achieved the scoring heights with the Maple Leafs and was the youngest player in the NHL when he joined Toronto. He really wanted to go to college but was talked out of it. After his stint with the Maple Leafs, he quit to go to college when Tommy Ivan obtained his rights and urged him to play for Chicago.

Nester told Tommy he wanted to stay in college and agreed to play only on the weekends. Eric appeared in only 24 games that season and scored eight goals.

Defensive Specialist

Eric's longevity in the NHL was a result of his defensive abilities. He was a strong skater, and with his size, Coach Reay assigned him to cover the opponents' best wingers. Also, he teamed up with Bill Hay as one of the most effective penalty-killing duos in the league. In fact, he was the first Hawk to score two shorthand goals in a game when he tallied twice against Montreal at the Stadium on March 7, 1965, during a 7-0 win over the Canadiens. That effort has been matched a half-dozen times since then by Hawks, but never surpassed.

Nesterenko has shadowed such stars in the '60s as Toronto's Frank Mahovlich, New York's Andy Bathgate, and

Montreal's Bernie Geoffrion. Eric constantly frustrated those stars. Nester—or "swoop," as some fans called him because of the way he skated—was not a fighter nor was he considered a dirty player. Nester averaged a penalty minute for every game he played for the Hawks (1,012).

Profound Reader

When I traveled with the team on charter flights, Eric and Bill Hay usually sat together and always seemed to be reading. Not that they weren't friendly, they just enjoyed reading. Eric told how exciting it was to play in the Chicago Stadium and he remembers how deafening the crowd noise was and how there was no place like it in the NHL. Since his retirement from hockey, he took up skiing and became an instructor in Colorado, but he hasn't had any more movie offers since *Youngblood.*

Ivan "Not Terrible" Boldirev

General manager Tommy Ivan got center Ivan Bolidrev in a trade from the California Golden Seals in 1974. Boldidrev played five seasons and led the Hawks in scoring his last three before getting involved in what was probably the second biggest trade in recent team history after the one that involved Phil Esposito and Pit Martin in 1967. He told me the trade to Atlanta in 1979 for Tom Lysiak and others upset him because playing in Chicago was a thrill.

Custom-Made Suits

When the players were in Montreal, a lot of them went to a certain tailor to get suits made at a reasonable cost. Ivan remembers one time when he got his suit he saw a very loud sports coat at the shop. He told the tailor that he would never wear a jacket like that.

On the same night after the game, he saw one of his teammates wearing the loud sports coat, but never said a word about it.

Curfew Violation Doesn't Pay!

Chicago was in Montreal to face the Canadiens and it was Chris Chelios's second trip to the Forum since the trade, so he was a bit nervous about the game. To help ease the anxiety, Cheli and fellow teammate Steve Smith hit the town the night before to relax. Time escaped them when they realized it was past the team's curfew, so they quickly headed back to the hotel. As the elevator door opened, there stood coach Keenan. He gave the pair a quick stare and walked past them.

At the morning skate Keenan said nothing to them, nor was anything said at the team's meeting and pregame meal.

Smith said to Cheli, "Is it possible he didn't see us?" Cheli shook his head.

Again, at game time during the warmup, Keenan said nothing. Smith and Cheli began to wonder if they might see little ice time, or worse yet, maybe Keenan would sit them out the whole game. But to their surprise, they both were slated to start.

The game was nearly two minutes old when they both headed to the bench after a whistle. Keenan stood at the bench door stone-faced, and pointed his finger at them to stay on the ice. A few more minutes and another whistle sent Smith and Chelios heading back to the bench, but yet again they were turned away by Keenan. The first period wore on as Smith and Chelios realized their curfew punishment: playing almost 40 exhausting minutes with little rest, and a 4-2 loss to Montreal.

Memorable Fight

Boston had a feisty player in Derek "bad boy" Sanderson in the late 1960s who tried to slow up Bobby Hull in various games. The Hawks were battling the Bruins through most of the '69-70 season for first place, which was finally decided on the last game of the season.

In February at the stadium, the two teams squared off and emotions were running high. The Hawks had a defenseman, Ray McKay, who was basically a rookie. He was tall and gangly, while Sanderson was less than six feet tall. Sanderson gave McKay an elbow as the two collided near the Hawk blue line and Sanderson starting swinging at the taller McKay. Sanderson tried to pull McKay's jersey off, but in the process fell, and McKay wound up on top while Sanderson was tied in the jersey. McKay delivered a few punches to the delight of the cheering Stadium and was declared the winner of the brawl.

McKay played only 28 games for the Hawks in three seasons with one assist and 35 penalty minutes. Sanderson played 13 seasons with five different teams in 598 games, but compiled 911 penalty minutes. It was McKay's only NHL fight, but he came out a winner!

Denis Savard

There's no doubt that the most exciting Blackhawk player since the departure of Bobby Hull and the retirement of Stan Mikita was Denis Savard ("Savvy"). Chicago got lucky in the 1980 draft in the same way the Chicago Bulls were when they drafted Michael Jordan. Portland selected Sam Bowie first and the Bulls wound up with a gem in Jordan. Montreal had the first overall pick and selected Doug Wickenheiser. Winnipeg needed a defenseman and selected Dave Babych second, while the Hawks got the real diamond in selecting Savard third overall.

Number 18 Jersey Retired

Savard's number 18 jersey is the fifth and most recent Hawk to have his number retired. Savvy was honored at the United Center on March 19, 1998, before the team played Montreal. Appropriately, the Hawks won that game 1-0 behind Jeff Hackett in goal. In June 2000, Savard became the newest Hawk to be inducted into the Hockey Hall of Fame.

Savard is fourth on the Hawk all-time goal list, third

in points behind Mikita and Hull, and second in assists to Mikita. In Stanley Cup play, Savard is second in the same three categories plus leads in hat tricks with three and got the first four-goal game by a Hawk in postseason play. His 131-point total in 1987-88 is also a team mark. Twice he had 87 assists in one season, 1981-82 and 1987-88.

Savvy's high-goal mark was 47 in 1985-86. His total regular-season marks place him among the top 25 in NHL history and top 12 in playoffs. Despite all his impressive statistics, he was only named to the All-Star team once, in 1982-83. In his rookie season (1980-81), he finished with 28 goals and 75 points, one behind team leader Tom Lysiak. He was edged out for the Calder Trophy for top rookie honors in very close voting to Boston's Ray Bourque and Detroit's Mike Foligno.

Savard's magic clicked when he teamed up with Steve Larmer and Al Secord in '82-83. That line set a club record of 132 goals and 297 points in the season. Secord scored 54 goals, Larmer 43 goals and Savvy 35. The team went to the conference finals for the second straight season.

Painful Trade

Savard played for 10 seasons before being traded to Montreal for Chris Chelios, where he was on the 1993 Stanley Cup championship team. After three seasons, he signed with Tampa Bay. After two seasons with the Lightning, general manager Phil Esposito gave Savard a chance to rejoin the Hawks in a trade. Savvy returned April 6 and went on to spark the Hawks in the playoffs with seven goals and 11 assists.

Spinning Frenchman!

Some labeled Savard the "Flying Frenchman," but I would call him the "spinning Frenchman." He made many spectacular goals with an unbelievable "spin-o-rama move" by holding onto the puck and doing a 360-degree turn, leaving a defender baffled and then firing a shot past an opposing goalie. In a game against Edmonton while short-handed, Savard stole the puck in his zone and proceeded to skate through the entire Oiler team and put the puck past goalie Grant Fuhr.

Stunning Comeback!

One of the great regular-season comebacks came in 1987 against the Oilers at the Stadium with the Hawks trailing 4-1 in the third period with less than eight minutes to play. Many of the fans began to leave when Savard set up Secord to cut the margin to 4-2. Then the tide swung as Chicago tallied three more to take the lead and then add an empty-netter to cap a 6-4 win against the visitors, who went on to win the Stanley Cup in '87. Earlier in the season, the Oilers had whipped Chicago 9-1. In January, Secord set a team record against Toronto by scoring four goals in the second period in eight minutes and 41 seconds—the fastest four by any Hawk, which only magnifies Mosienko's accomplishment of three goals in 21 seconds 25 years earlier. Secord became the second Hawk to score 50 goals in a season when he notched 54 in '82-83.

Rookie Season
Sees Number 21 Retire

Savard's first year was memorable in many ways, as he was on hand October 19, 1980, when the Hawks retired their first jersey in team history to honor Stan Mikita's number 21. It was 18 years later when number 18—Savard's jersey—was retired.

Savard Meets a Wood Chopper

Savvy didn't speak a lot of English in his rookie campaign, and he told his parents he was determined to make the team. Veterans always liked to play pranks on the newcomers.

In training camp, competition was fierce, and coach Keith Magnuson split the players into four teams for a round-robin tourney. Savvy paced his squad in scoring, and going into the "title" game, they were the favorites. Veteran defenseman Dave Hutchison was in his second season in Chicago after playing for Los Angeles and Toronto. He decided the only way his team could win would be to find a way to stop this sharp rookie. Each player had three sticks on the bench, which is usually more than enough for a game. Savard went out for his first shift and when he got the puck and took a shot, his stick broke in half. He went back to the bench to get his second stick, but again it broke. On his next shift he used his last stick and the results were identical. Savard had to go back to the dressing room to prepare more of his sticks, which all players prepare to suit their taste. It took Savvy most of the game to get back into action with new sticks, but it wasn't in time to win the training camp title with Hutchison being the culprit in sawing the sticks.

Returning to Chicago!

Denis told me that he has had many thrills in his career. Naturally, winning the Stanley Cup with Montreal was big, but coming back to the Hawks in '95 was a great feeling when he slipped a Blackhawk jersey back on. He scored in his first game back and went on to lead the team in scoring during the playoffs as Chicago went to the conference finals before losing to Detroit.

Late for Lunch? You Pay!

Another rookie initiation for Savard occurred when the team met for lunch after practice at an Oak Brook location. The deal was that the last player to show up bought the first round of drinks for the rest of the team. Doug Wilson told Savard that the lunch was at 1:30 and to be on time; meanwhile the rest of the squad got there by 1 p.m. Naturally, Savard was the last one there, and his teammates started ordering expensive drinks. Before sitting down for lunch, Savvy was given the bill for almost $400. He only had about $50 on him and no credit cards when they told him it was only a joke.

When in Las Vegas, Hit Me!

During a west coast swing, the team took a little break with a side trip to Las Vegas. It was Savard's first trip there, and his teammates gave him a few pointers on how to play blackjack. Savard was doing pretty good at the table, and his confidence was growing when he got dealt two queens while the dealer was showing a "7." Denis said, "Hit me." The dealer questioned him, and Doug Wilson tried to help him, but Savard insisted, "Hit me!" The dealer replied, "Did you want to split them?" Denis said, "No!" Then the dealer called over a pit boss who again questioned Denis and Savvy held his ground. The dealer hit Savard's hand with a "9" and the pit boss said, "That's the highest hand in Vegas history!"

If Not for the Oilers, the '80s Could Have Been Different

Denis feels—like many of his teammates through the 1980s —that they were very close to bringing back the Stanley Cup to Chicago. Edmonton, with Wayne Gretzky and crew, stopped them in the conference finals in '83, '85 and '90. The Oilers lost in the finals when the Islanders captured their fourth straight cup but won it five other times in that period.

886 Straight Games

Steve Larmer played for the Hawk minor league team in New Brunswick where the head coach was Orval Tessier. Larmer tallied 38 goals, while the team won the AHL Calder Cup.

The next season Tessier became head coach for the Hawks and he found a spot for the 22 year old who was a left-hand shot, but played the right side. The durable Larmer did not miss in his next 884 games—a team record and third highest in NHL history behind Doug Jarvis (964) and Gary Unger (914).

Larmer Records

Larmer ranks third in goals for the Hawks (406), fourth in points (923) and fifth in assists (517). In Stanley Cup play, Larmer is fourth in goals, assists and points. He led the team in scoring three straight years ('88-91) including 101 points in '90-91. He holds the Hawks' right wing scoring marks, and in his first season had 43 goals and 47 assists for 90 points to capture NHL Rookie of the Year honors.

The line of Larmer, Savard and Secord set a team record for a line in scoring 297 points, which still stands. Secord had been picked up in a trade with Boston in December for Chicago-born Mike O'Connell. Secord was a first-round draft pick for the Bruins in 1978, but had been up and down to the minors and Boston until the trade. With Larmer and Savard, Secord clicked and scored 213 goals in his eight seasons in Chicago. Larmer told me he appreciates the opportunity Tessier gave him to play for the Hawks. Ludzik gave Larmer the nickname "Gramps" when they were playing together in juniors. The easygoing Larmer liked peace and quiet, which is why Ludzik gave him the tag that stuck with him.

Superman!

Larmer didn't talk a lot and he let his actions on the ice speak for themselves. He played both ends of the ice, working on penalty killing and power plays. As far as the media were concerned, Larmer was called "Superman." After a game, Larmer would shower, dress and get out of the locker room quicker than "Superman" in order to avoid talking to the press.

Although he wasn't a practical joker, his roommate, Ludzik, always tried a few pranks. In preseason, the team had three games in three nights and had a fourth in a row coming up. Ludzik pushed the clock ahead a few hours, then woke up Larmer to tell him he overslept and missed the game.

Picture This

Defenseman Marc Bergevin was a third-round draft selection in 1983, and the 19-year-old Montreal native made the 1984 team. Pranks played on rookies in the '80s were different from the famed "snipe hunts" of the late 1960s.

Bergevin was not married and suddenly was getting mail from several different women. They sent pictures, usually in

Steve Larmer

bathing suits or scanty lingerie, saying they wanted to meet him. Bergevin was bragging to his teammates about the letters and pictures until they finally told him the truth.

Fast Puck, but Where's It Going?

Steve recalls Winger Ken Yaremchuk who was a first-round pick in 1983 and was very speedy in his three seasons in Chicago. In practice, Kenny was very active. In fact, veteran goalie Tony Esposito would leave his net when Yaremchuk started carrying the puck. He could fire a puck almost 100 miles per hour but never seemed to know where it was going!

Charity Time

Despite being shy, I remember the many times that Larmer, Savard, Darryl Sutter and Doug Wilson gave up their free time to accompany me to visit veterans' hospitals and cheer up the hospitalized veterans for the Bedside Network.

Hawk Fans Recognize Larmer's Feats

Larmer's statistics earned him the No.1 right wing spot on the Blackhawk 75th anniversary team ahead of Bill Mosienko and Jim Pappin. In most of the key scoring categories, Larmer is in the top four during regular season and playoffs. When you add in that he played in 884 straight games while playing the right side instead of his natural left side, his accomplishments stand out even more. He played in two All-Star games and while on Team Canada in the 1991 Canada Cup, he scored the winning goal in the series against Team USA.

Darryl Sutter

Steve was traded in 1993 in a three-team deal that landed him in New York with the Rangers when they won the Stanley Cup with his former Hawk coach Mike Keenan. When he retired, he had played in 1,006 games and earned 1,012 points. I feel his accomplishments certainly will earn him a spot in the Hockey Hall of Fame and after that hopefully his No. 28 jersey will be hoisted in the United Center alongside the other Chicago offensive greats Mikita, Hull and Savard. "Gramps" deserves that honor!

Stan Mikita: The Ultimate Blackhawk

There have been a lot of words written and said about Stan Mikita ("Stash"), but I like what former teammate, Hall of Famer and three-time Norris Trophy winner Pierre Pilote told me: "Pound for pound, Stan was the best. He was durable and tough. He could kill penalties, set up plays, and fake a goalie out of his skates and score!"

Mikita Captures Three Trophies Two Years in a Row

"Stash" owns or shares 15 Blackhawk regular-season and playoffs scoring records. He was and still is the only player in NHL history to win the Art Ross Trophy (scoring), Hart Trophy (most valuable player) and Lady Byng Trophy (sportsmanship) all in one season—and he did it twice (1966-67 and 1967-68). Also, he won the scoring title two other times and was named to the All-Star team eight times.

Mikita played for 22 seasons, getting 541 goals, 926 assists for 1,467 points in 1,394 games plus 59 goals, and 91 assists for 150 playoff points in 155 playoff matches. His No. 21 jersey was the first ever retired by the Hawks on October 19, 1980, and he was elected to the Hockey Hall of Fame in 1983.

Biggest Thrill

Stan told me of his many thrills as a Blackhawk, including the 1961 Stanley Cup, award trophies, All-Star games, and the retirement of his jersey. Stan rates having his oldest son, Scott, introduce him at the Hall of Fame ceremonies as the biggest thrill of all!

Mikita was the first Slovak-born player to make it to the NHL. He started with the Hawk junior team, St. Catharine's, where Rudy Pilous had coached before coming to Chicago to eventually lead the Hawks to the Stanley Cup in 1961.

A Lot of Fight in a Small Package

Mikita was not big, weighing only about 165 pounds, and he knew rookies were always being tested. He wanted to prove that he belonged. Veteran Ted Lindsay, who had played in Detroit with Gordie Howe and had four Stanley Cup rings, told the rookie if he wanted to last in the NHL, he must hit the other guy first.

In his first season, Mikita led the team in penalty minutes with 119, and in three of the next five seasons he had 97-plus minutes. Lindsay told Stan he'd need an extra-long stick to score from the penalty box. The scrappy Lindsay had compiled more than 1,800 penalty minutes during his career in 1,068 games, but still managed to score 379 goals, mostly playing with Howe and Alex Delvecchio in Detroit.

From the Penalty Box to More Goals

Mikita established himself as a gritty player in his first six seasons and in 1963-64, he had a career-high 39 goals and 50 assists to lead the Hawks and the NHL in scoring and spent 146 minutes in the penalty box, which also led the team, edging out Reggie Flemming's 140 minutes. The following season, Stan again led the team and league in scoring with

87 points and hit a career high in penalty minutes (154) but captain Pierre Pilote spent eight more minutes in the penalty box (162). In '65-66, Mikita cut his time in the penalty box almost in half (58), but saw teammate Hull grab league-scoring honors when the Golden Jet became the first player to score more than 50 goals in a season twice with 54.

Mikita Repeats Trio of Trophies

The next two seasons ('66-67 and '67-68), Mikita again led the team and NHL in scoring to lead the Hawks and reduced his penalty minutes to only 12 and 14. Goalie Glenn Hall told Stan, "I guess the other teams got tired of trying to kill you each night, and you didn't have to retaliate." Stan's drastic reduction of penalty time earned him the Lady Byng Trophy for sportsmanship those two years, in addition to the Ross Trophy and Hart Trophy. Stan not only became the first and only NHL player to win all three trophies in one season, but he did it two seasons straight.

Haircut and a Close Shave

In training camp during his fourth season, coach Pilous required all players to be clean-shaven, and their hair had to be a certain length or fines were in order. Considering what salaries were then, Mikita needed to get a haircut before the next day. After the afternoon practice, Stan was going to the barber shop, but veterans Len Lunde and Wayne Hillman persuaded him to join them for some liquid refreshment, telling him he had time to go to the barber.

A few hours later Stan found the shop closed. Lunde told him not to worry because he had an electric clipper back in his hotel room. At that point, Stan was a little desperate, even though both Lunde and Hillman couldn't walk a straight line. They got to the room and sat Stan down as Lunde proceeded to start clipping. "Whoops," Lunde said to Stan, "Don't worry, the clipper slipped a bit, but I'll even it out on other side." Then Lunde started clipping the other side with the same comments. Stan said by the time Lunde got done, he had shaved off all but the hair just on the top of his head. Fortunately, it must have helped Stan's speed, because it turned out to be his best season yet in 1962-63 as he led the team in scoring for the first time and matched Hull in goals with 31. The following season, he won the NHL scoring title and improved his season goal total to his best (39).

Extra Stitches Means Extra $$$

The Hawk trainer in those days was Nick Garen and when players received cuts, it was the trainer's job to do the stitches. Later, the league required doctors to be on hand for that first aid.

Mikita got a small cut during a game, and he needed Nick to take care of him. Garen promptly applied seven stitches and Stan said, "Why did I need that many stitches for my cut?" Nick replied, "We get an paid extra $5 for every stitch!"

Get Me to the Airport

There was another rule in the '60s that players could report to training camp and play in preseason games, but unless they signed their contracts, they couldn't start the season.

In 1965, Mikita had come off two straight seasons of leading the NHL and Hawks in scoring, and was having trouble negotiating a new deal with GM Tommy Ivan. The team was in Toronto for the last preseason game and Stan told Ivan that if he didn't have a contract done by 6 p.m., he was going back to Chicago; he wasn't going to play another year for practically nothing.

It was close to six when Stan took his bag and was going to take the bus to the airport to save money instead of taking a cab. There were four other people on the bus, and the driver was ready to pull out when a bell boy came out of the hotel calling for Mikita, saying there was a phone call in the lobby. Mikita stepped out of the bus to take the call. It was Tommy Ivan, who asked Mikita to come up to his room. Mikita said he was taking the bus to the airport. Ivan told him he would pay him for a taxi after they talked. Stan went up to the room, but left his suitcase in the door when he entered, so he could leave in a hurry. Tommy said, "Are you ready to negotiate?" Stan replied, "I feel I deserve a raise." The wily GM said, "You got a $500 raise last year, and we're paying you enough now."

Stan got up and headed to the door. Tommy then said, "I'll have to call Mr. [Jim] Norris."

Stan waited as Tommy went into the next room to call the Hawk owner, who was in Florida.

Tommy was in a loud conversation and came back to tell Stan he couldn't give him any more money. Stan said, "Let me talk to Mr. Norris." Tommy said he couldn't do it, because he wouldn't be able to reach him. Again, Stan was heading out and he asked Tommy for the cab fare. Ivan relented and said he would call Mr. Norris back, but Stan said, "Give me his number and I will call him from a pay phone in the lobby." When Tommy saw that Stan wouldn't back off, he gave him the Florida phone number.

Stan went downstairs and made the call and came back to the room to tell him that Mr. Norris approved a new deal.

Five Straight 30-Plus Goal Seasons

Armed with a new contract, Stan had another terrific season with 30 goals and 48 assists but finished second in league scoring to teammate Hull, who had 54 goals. Mikita rattled off two more league scoring titles, and had five straight 30-plus goal seasons and still holds the team mark for 14 straight 20-plus goal seasons as his Chicago career encompassed 22 seasons.

In his career, he played with many of the Hawk greats like Hull, Bobby and Dennis, Glenn Hall, Tony Esposito, Phil Esposito, Pilote, Ted Lindsay, Kenny Wharram, Bill White, Pat Stapleton, Doug Wilson and Pit Martin to mention a few. In addition, he played against Maurice "Rocket" Richard, Jean Beliveau, Doug Harvey, Terry Sawchuk, Gordie Howe, Bobby Orr, Frank Mahovlich, Jacques Plante, Red Kelly and Guy LaFleur.

Psychology

Mikita feels that Billy Reay was a "hell" of a coach who knew how to read his players and used a psychological approach to motivate. Stan remembers one game in which the team played a lousy first period and were getting beat. The coach delayed his appearance in the locker room between periods. Just before they were to go back on the ice for the second period, Reay came in and starting shouting at his players. He singled out his two stars: Mikita and Hull. He told his players, "Don't expect these guys to bail you out every game. They weren't too hot in the last period, either! Now let's go out there and do something!" As the players headed up the stairs to the ice, Reay pulled Mikita and Hull back and whispered to them, "Do you think my speech will get them going?" Apparently it did, as the team went on to rally and win the game.

Where's My Radio?

Just before the Hawks were facing the California Seals at the Chicago Stadium on November 22, 1970, coach Reay handed Stan a letter and asked him to read it to the team. The Seals had just changed their name from Oakland in midseason, and the Hawks had beaten them 5-1 in the season opener. Mikita started reading the sob-story letter from an older woman who said she was an avid Blackhawks fan, and although she couldn't afford to come to the games, she would listen to the games on the radio. She said she was a widow and that her children lived out of town. Stan told me he was starting to cry as he was reading the letter. The woman said she couldn't listen anymore because someone stole her radio. Stan turned the page and the woman's last words were, "I hope you guys find that S.O.B. who stole my radio, so I can hear the games again!"

Billy Reay's psychology apparently worked as the Hawks went out and blanked the Seals 9-0 as Hull got the hat trick!

Take the "A" Train

When there were just six teams, the road trips were mainly made by train as opposed to chartered planes and commercial airlines. This made for closer knit situations among the players. Also, with a number of characters, there were many pranks and comedy routines.

Defenseman Doug Jarrett and Dennis Hull used to team up with their version of Abbott and Costello. Although it may lose something in the translation after many years, Stan recalled one routine this way: Doug would say, "I'll climb a mountain!" and Dennis would reply, "Ever Rest?" "Not until I get to the top!" as Jarrett got in the last line.

The Scooter Line

Ab McDonald was the steady winger as part of the famed "scooter line" with Mikita and Wharram in 1960-61 while Bobby Hull, Bill Hay and Murray Balfour had the title of the "million-dollar line." The "scooters" had 61 goals, 71 goals and 92 goals in three seasons before McDonald was traded.

Veteran Doug Mohns, a defenseman, was picked up from Boston in a trade in December 1964. The following season, Coach Reay put Mohns on a line with Mikita and Wharram, and the line clicked for 78 goals. Then they tallied 91 goals in each of the next two campaigns and 82 in '68-69 before Wharram retired.

Thin on Top?

Mohns was a little self-conscious about being bald, and he started wearing a helmet plus a hair piece. On a road trip when they were going through an airport, the playful Pat Stapleton stuck a sign on the back of Mohns's coat saying, "I'm wearing a rug," with an arrow pointing to his head.

People walked behind Mohns, and others passed him, chuckling before Doug found out about it.

Howie Young: Ride 'em Cowboy

Stan remembers Howie Young used to ride his motorcycle up and down the stairs to the locker room at the Chicago Stadium. The talented Young had two seasons with the Hawks. Also, Stan regards Eric Nesterenko as the NHL's first "hippie" hockey player during his Hawk career.

Cliff Koroll: A Stitch in Time?

Denver University contributed to the Hawks in 1969 when Cliff Koroll made the team after a year with the Central Hockey League team in Dallas in 1968, as he joined Keith Magnuson and Jim Wiste.

Koroll spent 11 seasons with the Hawks and finished with 208 goals as he eventually wound up on a line with Stan Mikita and then became an assistant coach.

Although he did not major in medicine, he got an early taste in his pro career. On his first road trip with Dallas into Omaha, one of his teammates told him, "If you get cut here, make it early." Cliff didn't know what he meant, but found out when there was about a minute left in the game. He got a bad cut and needed stitches.

The game ended and the trainer sent him across the ice to the first aid room to await a doctor. Cliff laid on a table for more than 20 minutes when he heard someone coming. He looked down the hall and saw this figure staggering down the hall—it was the doctor.

Cliff said he was reeking from alcohol and told him to lie still as he started stitching.

Cliff was in a little bit of shock as he got back to the team hotel and tried to go to sleep. He got into bed, but couldn't close his cut eye because the doctor had sewed his eyelid to his eyebrow.

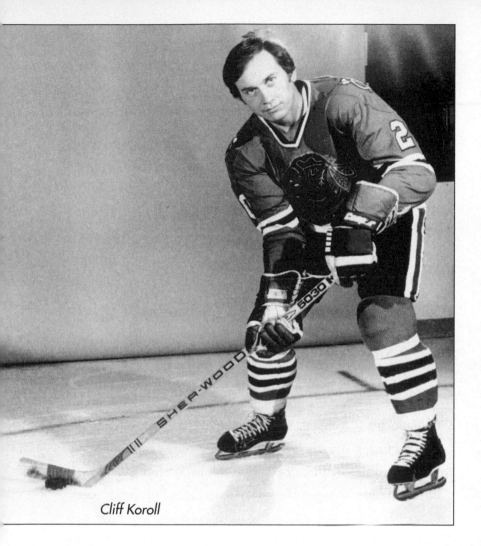

Cliff Koroll

Hold That Phone...Line

Cliff's luck with doctors didn't get a lot better when he joined the Hawks in Chicago. He got a cut inside his mouth and needed stitches. The Chicago doctor came down to the locker room to stitch Cliff up. He kept getting interrupted as he was working on Cliff and then left in a hurry to answer a phone call. However, he forgot to sew up the stitches, and he still held the needle as he began to drag Cliff down the hall with the stitches in his mouth. Ouch!

Negotiations

Cliff had a good season and a college degree, so he asked for a raise of $500 to $8,500 from the general manager. Tommy told him, "If you don't like what I'm offering, go out and get a job!"

Salaries Jump, and Players Too

The '70s were a good decade for the Blackhawks, and Cliff, as many echoed, would have been a lot better if the World Hockey Association hadn't come along. The new hockey league and the signing of Bobby Hull away from the Hawks for $2 million changed the salary structure of players forever. Not only did it lure one of the most exciting players ever to play the game away from Chicago, six other Hawk players also jumped to the new league. Although the Hawks did make it to the Stanley Cup finals in 1973, the loss of depth prevented a chance to win another cup, and Chicago did not return to the finals again until 1992.

Trainers: Unheralded but Necessary

When a Hawk player goes down on the ice, the first person off the bench is the trainer. The Hawks have been fortunate to have capable men that most fans hardly notice. When I got involved, the trainer was Nick Garen who passed away in 2002. Nick was from the New York area and was in charge when the team won the Stanley Cup in 1961. He left in 1969 to return to his hometown area and work for the Rangers.

Hawk goalie great Glenn Hall told me his favorite Nick Garen story. Glenn asked Nick how old he was. The trainer replied, "Forty. I would have been 42, but I was sick for two years."

From Stitches to Steaks

Garen was replaced by Charles "Skip" Thayer who served as trainer for 18 seasons before the current trainer, Mike Gapski took over and is beginning his 17th season.

The favorite Skip Thayer story occurred in Denver when he went out with several of the players to a steak house that was offering a "special." If you finished their 48-ounce steak, you got a second one free! You guessed it, Skip ate the first one and then knocked off the second one! However, Skip did "skip" dessert!

Don't Slam That Door

Mike Gapski—or as the players call him, "Gapper"—has realized a lifelong dream by being the team trainer and is the first Chicago-born resident to hold the position. Mike served as trainer for the NHL All-Star game in 1991 and also for Team Canada in the 1991 Canada Cup.

Gapper recalls in his first year (1987) when Bob Murdoch was head coach and the team was playing in St. Louis at the old arena. Chicago was behind after the first period, and Murdoch and his assistants were upset. The coaches' room was down the hall from the players' locker room. The players were waiting to get the verbal blasts from the staff in the locker room, but the coaches never showed up, and the intermission ended and the Hawks went back on the ice. It seems that in a fit of rage, Murdoch slammed the door and the lock jammed, trapping the coaches. It wasn't until midway through the second period that the coaches were freed, but it was too late to turn the tide in that game against the Blues. Temper, temper, temper!

Keenan's Halloween Night

No one could ever accuse Hawk coach Mike Keenan of not being intense during the hockey season and especially during the heat of a game. It was Halloween night, 1989, when the Hawks were winding up a road trip in Calgary during Keenan's first season behind the Chicago bench. The Hawks had beaten Edmonton the night before, but were off to 3-8-1 start.

The first period was frightful, and the Flames built up an early lead. In the locker room after the period ended, Keenan was ready to scare the ghosts out his team! He was turning red with anger and spied what he thought was an empty bucket. He went to kick it across the room, but to his surprise, it was filled with pucks and he broke his toe! His pain was not eased as the Hawks lost to Calgary 6-3. At least in the next few seasons, he stopped kicking buckets and concentrated more on kicking a few of his players' butts!

Bobby Hull: Excitement Plus

Chicago hockey fans have been blessed with some of the greatest players of all time. There are currently seven jerseys, and most belong in the all time great category. Every time all-time NHL teams are named, the left wing is Bobby Hull! There has never been a player who could generate excitement like the Golden Jet. Hull holds 16 regular season Hawk records and eight playoff records. With his brother, Dennis, who ranks fifth in all-time Hawk goal scorers, the two brothers tallied 913 in the NHL—11 better than the next brother duo, Maurice and Henri Richard. The only brother group higher are the six Sutters (1,320). With his son, Brett, they have the highest father-son combo in league annuals (1,351) which even tops the Sutter clan. I'm proud to know Bobby for more than 50 years and have been fortunate to see him during his great Hawk career and his accomplishments speak for themselves.

Hardest Shot—
With or Without a Hook

Hull and Mikita both developed curved hockey sticks during their careers. For Mikita, it allowed him to produce some dips and spins. For Hull, with 120-mile-per-hour shots, it added more fear for goalies.

In 1969, the NHL changed the rules to limit the curves to one inch because of Hull and Mikita.

Glenn Hall told me that Bobby had the hardest shot he ever faced, mostly in practice until he was picked up by St. Louis in the expansion draft. Dennis also had a hard, heavy shot, but didn't possess the accuracy of Bobby.

Bobby always put fans first, especially on the road trips. Bobby was the last one on the bus, because he always tried to satisfy fans who wanted autographs.

With his speed and power, he would wind up behind his net and move up ice while avoiding checks or virtually carrying opponents on his back to score. No matter who his linemates were, Hull would tell them, "When you see me open, just get the puck on my stick!" Hull had a simple philosophy, "If you want to score, you'd better shoot a lot!"

Changing Numbers: 16-7-9!

As a rookie joining the Hawks in 1957, Hull was given No. 16. The youngster wound up the season with 13 goals and

34 assists to finish second in points on the team behind captain Ed Litzenberger. Hull finished second for rookie of the year honors, with first place going to Toronto's Frank Mahovlich.

Hull wore No.16 until Christmas 1961 when the Hawks faced Toronto at the Stadium. When he got to his locker, the No. 7 jersey was hanging instead of No.16. Hull had been struggling with only 13 goals after 31 games after getting 31 in the Stanley Cup '60-61 season and 39 the year before. He asked assistant trainer and backup goalie, Walter "Gunzo" Humeniuk, where No.16 was. Gunzo replied, "This should change your luck!" Ted Lindsay had worn that number in the 1959-60 season. Before Hull wore No.16, Johnny Wilson had the number in '56-57. Chico Maki joined the Hawks later in the season and wore No.18, but eventually switched to No.16 and played with Bobby.

The Gunzo jersey switch for Bobby worked its magic as he scored 37 goals the rest of the season to hit 50 goals for the first time in his career, matching the NHL record of Montreal's Rocket Richard and Bernie Geoffrion.

Gunzo wasn't through with Bobby and his jerseys. As I mentioned, besides being assistant trainer, Gunzo had served as backup goalie in the days when teams dressed only one goalie.

Gunzo faced the Hawks in practice, especially since Glenn Hall didn't want to take shots from Bobby, Mikita, Hay and Ron Murphy. In 1962-63, teams started dressing two goalies each game. Gunzo later opened a number of sporting goods stores and supplied the team's equipment.

Number 9 Begins

It was at the start of the 1963-64 season when the Hawks opened at home against the New York Rangers, and Hull found the No. 9 jersey in his locker stall. The number had been last worn by Todd Sloan in 1961 when the Hawks won the Cup.

Bobby asked Gunzo about the switch again. Gunzo said, "You're better than those other guys wearing 9." Gunzo was referring to Detroit's Gordie Howe and Montreal's Rocket Richard.

Bobby's goal total went up to 43 with four hat tricks that season. The following campaign, Hull scored 39 goals, but missed nine games due to knee injuries. His brother Dennis joined the team and had 10 goals. The 1965-66 season saw Bobby win the NHL scoring title for the third time and clicked for his second 50-plus goal total (54) while missing five games. Bobby's No. 9 jersey became the second in Hawk history to be retired in 1983.

Bobby told me he has had many thrills. "I achieved my boyhood dream by playing in the NHL and winning the Stanley Cup in 1961. Getting 500 goals and being named to the Hockey Hall of Fame are high on my list. I'll never forget the ovation from the fans at the Stadium on March 2, 1966, when I scored my 50th goal for the second time." I had to wait for several minutes to make the official announcement of Hull's goal, and the delay lasted many minutes.

The Hawks were shut out the next three games before facing the Rangers at the Stadium 10 days later on March

12. It was five and a half minutes into the third period when Lou Angotti fed Hull a pass, and the famous No. 9 blasted his record-setting 51st goal past Cesare Maniago.

As wild as the crowd was 10 days earlier when Hull got his 50th, this surpassed it.

Hats were thrown on the ice, and there was a 10-minute delay. I don't know if the 20,000-plus fans were able to hear my goal announcement. Bobby told me he had goose bumps and wanted to find someplace to hide. "I skated over to my bench to thank Louie (Angotti) for the pass, and he told me he had goose bumps, too."

Bobby added three more goals before the end of the season for a record-breaking 54.

More Milestones for Number 9

It was exactly one year later, March 12, 1967, that Hull contributed to another Hawk mark in the last season of a six-team league.

The Hawks hosted the Toronto Maple Leafs at the Stadium. Hull scored his 48th goal of the campaign when he blew a shot past goalie Terry Sawchuk. Although it did not top his record-breaking 51st goal of the year before, it contributed to the 5-0 victory over the Leafs to clinch the first first-place finish in Chicago's 41-year history! Hull added four more goals in the remaining nine games to wind up with 52 to register his third 50-plus goal campaign and become the first player to have back-to-back 50-plus seasons. Hull wound up second in league scoring to teammate Mikita.

Bobby had an off year in 1967-68 compared to his two straight 50-plus goal seasons, but he still was the top goal scorer in the league with 44. Again, Mikita took NHL scoring honors with 40 goals and 47 assists. It was the only time that Mikita scored 40 in his 22 Hawk seasons.

Hull, Hawk Scoring Record Fall but Team Finishes Last

With expansion in its second season in 1968-69, the loss of team depth took its toll on the Hawks. Team scoring records fell, and so did Chicago's standings. I called this team the best "last-place finishers." The Hawks wound up sixth in the East Division despite a winning record (34-33-9), which would have put them second in the expansion West Division.

Meanwhile, No. 9 broke his single-season scoring record with 58 goals, his fourth 50-plus year. The record-breaking 55th goal came at Boston on March 20, 1969. Hull scored his 54th and 55th goals 13 seconds apart late in the third period. The game wound up in a 5-5 tie when Bruins star Bobby Orr tallied with one second left in the game.

With five games left in the season, Bobby picked up two more going into the finale at the stadium against Detroit on March 30, 1969. The team had already clinched last place after tying the Wings the night before, who had a three-point lead. It was a wild game with the Hawks winning 9-5. Hull scored his record 58th goal and a Hawk-record 107 points for the season, but former teammate Phil Esposito won the Art Ross Trophy with 126 points, including 49 goals.

Detroit's Frank Mahovlich also had 49 goals and had a couple near misses in that final game at the stadium. Mikita had another great year with 97 points to finish fourth behind Gordie Howe's 103 points. In that last game, Pit Martin scored four goals, and Pat Stapleton got six assists in the second period to tie an NHL record for assists by defensemen in one period, which still stands.

Martin, as far as I know, is the first player to score four goals against the Hawks and four goals for the Hawks. He got the four-bagger against while with Boston.

Chicago set a host of team records despite the last-place finish: most goals scored in a season (280), five players with 30-plus goals, seven players with 20-plus goals, and Stapleton became the first Hawk blue liner to get more than 50 points in a season (6-50=56). That mark fell in 1981-82 when Doug Wilson scored 39 goals and had 46 assists for 85 points. Chris Chelios set the Hawk record for most assists by a defenseman in season (58) in 1992-93 and matched it again in '95-96.

Bobby Tries His Hand at TV

As Chicago missed the playoffs for the first time in 10 years, Bobby wound up as a commentator on the CBS TV hockey playoffs, but repeatedly said he would rather be on the ice playing, which he did the following year.

Bobby Holds Out

After his record-breaking season, Bobby sat out the first 15 games of 1969-70 in a contract dispute and threatened to ask for a trade. At the start of training camp, Pit Martin spoke out about a lack of team spirit and a lack of direction after the previous season's last-place finish. Another key loss before the start of the season came when Ken Wharram had to retire because of a heart condition. Wharram had 252 career goals and a speedy key on a line with Mikita, plus having five straight years of 24-plus goals.

The Hawks started out losing their first five games, tying the Rangers 1-1 in the fifth with Cliff Koroll getting his first NHL goal. The next game was in Montreal, and rookie goalie Tony Esposito faced his old team for the first time. Tony "O" got his first Hawk shutout, 5-0, and went on to 14 more that season for a modern-day shutout mark.

Meanwhile, Bobby announced he was retiring and going back to his cattle ranch in Canada. Rumors began circulating in the first week in November that Bobby was back and skating in the western suburbs. Former assistant trainer and back-up goalie Walter "Gunzo" Humeniuk, now a sporting goods store owner, was tending goal for Bobby late at night.

Finally the contract deadlock was resolved, and Bobby joined the team on November 10 for a game against the Rangers at the Stadium. Right after the national anthem, the fans started chanting, "Bobby! Bobby!" Coach Reay didn't send the Golden Jet out until near the five-minute mark. Bobby showed signs of rust and didn't score, and he had three shots on goal.

It wasn't until two games later at the stadium against Pittsburgh that the red light went on for Bobby. Pittsburgh was leading 2-1 early in the final period when Mikita threw a pass to Hull who fired a slap shot past goalie Al Smith for his first of the season.

The crowd roared its approval when I made the official announcement, "Blackhawk goal, his first of the season, scored by No. 9, Bobby Hull, assisted by No. 21, Stan Mikita and No. 7, Pit Martin at 5:53!" Hull's slow start due to the hold-out began to build momentum for the team, which seemed to come together more each game. The annual All-Star game was held in St. Louis in January, with the East Division against the West. The Hawks had gone into the break with a six-game win streak and were on the heels of Detroit for first place.

Hull, Tony Esposito and Mikita represented the Hawks in the All-Star game. Hull got a goal and an assist and was named the No. 1 star of the game. The first game after the break was in Detroit, and a Hawk win would pull them into first place and stretch their win streak to seven. Bobby scored in the final period to put the Hawks up 4-2 and resulted in being the winning goal in the 4-3 decision.

Hull's 500th Career Goal

The month of March had always been a good one for Bobby in breaking the 50-goal mark, but February was also one for Hull milestones.

The Hawks were battling for first place when GM Tommy Ivan pulled off a trade with last-place Los Angeles. With rookie Tony Esposito sparkling in the nets, Denis DeJordy was expendable, along with defensemen Gilles Marotte and Jim Stanfield. Chicago got goalie Gerry Desjardins, center Bryan Campbell, and one of the best defenseman in Bill White. The new players arrived in time for the Ranger game at the stadium February 21, 1970.

Hull had 26 goals for the season and 498 for his NHL career. Only two other players in league history had reached the 500 plateau: Montreal's Rocket Richard and Detroit's Gordie Howe.

The Hawks were trailing 2-0 near the midway point of the second period when Doug Mohns fired a shot that appeared to deflect off Hull on a power play. The official scorer told me to announce that Mohns got the goal, which I did. At the next stoppage of play, Mohns skated over to tell the official scorer and me that his shot went off Bobby. Then I announced the change, giving the Golden Jet 499 goals. Less than two minutes later, Hull tallied again, but this time it was brother Dennis to tie the game at two-all.

Defenseman White got a little bit of history nearly six minutes later when he fired the puck along the boards behind the Ranger net. Lou Angotti picked it up and flipped out in front of the goal where No. 9 banged it past goalie Ed Giacomin, and the stadium crowd erupted. Once again, I don't know if my voice carried over the noise when I announced, "Blackhawk goal, his 28th and 500th of his career, scored by

No. 9 Bobby Hull, assisted by No. 6 Lou Angotti and No. 2 Bill White at 16:51!" Hull's historic tally proved to be the game winner.

With 19 games left on the schedule, Hull added 10 more goals to wind up with 38 in 61 games, one less than teammate Mikita (39), but more importantly the Hawks won 14, tied two and lost only three while gaining first place in the last and crazy game in the season finale.

Must Win for First Place

April 5, 1970 was the game that the Hawks needed to win to edge out Boston for first place, and Montreal needed to win, tie or score five goals to beat out New York for the last playoff slot.

Although Montreal scored first, the Hawks took the lead late in the second period. Pit Martin got the hat trick—his first since the last game of the season before when he scored four goals.

The Canadiens were behind 5-2 when they pulled their goalie, and the Hawks got five empty-netters in the final 12 minutes. After finishing last in the east in the previous year, the Hawks jumped to first while knocking the Canadiens out of the postseason for the first time in 22 years. Rookie defenseman Keith Magnuson failed to score a goal even with the empty net as Gerry Pinder tallied the last goal in the closing seconds instead of passing to Keith.

There's Gold in the West Without the Hook

With Vancouver and Buffalo joining the league in '70-71, the Blackhawks moved over to the West Division where St. Louis—coached by Scotty Bowman—had reigned for two straight seasons with former Hawk goalie Glenn Hall.

Bobby Hull fell short of the 50-goal mark but still managed to break a few more records as he scored 44—third in the league behind Boston's Phil Esposito's record 76 and John Bucyk's 51 goals. Hull passed up Montreal's Rocket Richard's NHL career mark of 544 goals on Valentine's Day 1971 against Vancouver at the stadium.

Bobby didn't stop there.

A week later he scored the three-goal hat trick against Los Angeles at the stadium. It was his 27th hat trick, again eclipsing Richard's 26 hat tricks. Hawk coach Billy Reay, who played with Richard, said he thought he would never see that hat trick record broken. Hull ended his career with 28, which is now held by Wayne Gretzky (50).

The Hawks wound up the season in first in the West Division, but Hull and Mikita were deprived of their big hooks on their sticks; the league passed a rule limiting the size of the curve on the sticks.

Practice Makes Perfect

During his playing days with the Hawks, there were two things that goalie Glenn Hall hated: training camp and facing

Bobby's shots in practice.

Before the NHL rule in 1962 that required each team to dress two goalies for each game, Glenn preferred to have the assistant trainer, Gunzo, face those 100 mile-per-hour shots. Bobby liked to have fun while the cleaning crews were working in the stands by whistling shots into the seats to scatter them. His shots had the same effect on opposing goalies for 15 NHL seasons!

Hull's Fifth and Last 50-Goal Season for the Hawks

The Hawks were going for their third straight first place when the '71-72 season got underway. Few realized as Bobby Hull started his 15th season in Chicago that it would his last in Blackhawk uniform. His 28th and last hat trick in the NHL came in Oakland on December 22, 1971. Bobby registered his 600th career goal in Boston on March 25, 1972 in a 5-5 tie. It was the same day 10 years earlier that Hull got his first 50-goal season against New York.

Going into the final game of the season, the Hawks hosted Detroit at the Stadium, April 2,1972, and Hull had 48 goals as Chicago ran away with the West Division title by 21 points over Minnesota. A little more than three minutes into the game, Hull fired home his 49th goal.

Then with less than three minutes to go in the opening period, Chico Maki fed Bobby a pass, and in typical Hull fashion, his slap shot blew by the Red Wing goalie.

Once again the Stadium crowd exploded, and I made

the announcement, "Blackhawk goal, his 50th of the season, scored by No. 9, Bobby Hull, assisted by No.16 Chico Maki and No. 3 Keith Magnuson at 17:09!"

Little did I know, that goal number 604 by Hull would be the last regular-season one I would announce for Bobby.

Bobby's Last Playoff for the Hawks

In the playoffs, the Hawks met Pittsburgh for the first time in the playoffs. The Hawks took the first two at the stadium, and then Billy Reay started Gary Smith in goal to give Tony Esposito a rest, and Smith chalked up his only Hawk playoff shutout, 2-0, to give them a 3-0 edge in the best-of-seven series. The Penguins tried not to be swept and held a 4-2 lead in the third period. It took less than five minutes for Bobby to score twice for his second career playoff hat trick and his first in 10 years. Brother Dennis put the Hawks ahead midway in the period, but Pittsburgh tied the game with two minutes to play to send the game into overtime.

It took only 12 seconds when Pit Martin banged home the winner to sweep the series. It set an NHL record for the fastest overtime goal, which has since been broken but remains a Hawk mark.

Then it was time to face New York, who ousted Montreal. The Rangers had not forgotten the year before when the Hawks outlasted them in the seven classic game series in 1971. New York stunned the Hawks in the first two games at the stadium 3-2 and 5-3. Going back to Madison Square

Garden, the Rangers won 3-2, and then on April 23, 1972, they swept the Hawks 6-2.

Early in the first period, Hull got his first goal of the series on the type of play that excited Hawk fans and all hockey fans. Chicago was short handed as the puck squirted into center ice, Hull put on a burst of speed, took the puck away from the Ranger defender to move in on the goalie. Hull faked one way to move the goalie out of position and slipped the puck into the net. It was Bobby's lone goal of the series, his 62nd playoff goal and last in a Hawk uniform as he jumped to Winnipeg and the World Hockey Association the next season.

Bobby's playoff goal total (62) is still No. 1 among all Hawks, just ahead of Denis Savard (61) and Stan Mikita (59).

The loss of seeing Bobby's famous rink-long rushes and scoring goals was felt by Chicago fans and NHL fans for many seasons!

Silver Jet Would Have Been a Greater Star with a Different Last Name

If you ask most Hawk fans to name the team's all-time goal scorer, the names of Bobby Hull, Stan Mikita, Denis Savard and Steve Larmer will come up. Some may add Jeremy Roenick, Tony Amonte, Pit Martin and Billy Mosienko to the list.

You might be surprised to learn that Dennis Hull ranks fifth in goals with 298 and sixth in total points with 640. In playoff scoring, Dennis is sixth in goals and seventh in total points, just behind Roenick in both categories.

Coach Billy Reay calls Dennis "a great left wing." There's no doubt in my mind that Dennis would have been more highly regarded if he had a different last name. Although after Bobby left for the WHA in '72, Dennis wasn't expected to fill his skates, he clicked with Pit Martin and Jim Pappin to form the "M-P-H" line. Dennis scored 40 goals in '70-71, 30 in '71-72 and 39 in '72-73. The M-P-H line set a Hawk record in '72-73 when Pappin had 41 goals, Dennis 39 and Martin 29 with a point total of 272. That mark lasted for 10 years until it was broken by Savard, Larmer and Secord with 297 points.

Dennis played 13 seasons for Chicago before finishing his career in Detroit.

Second Hawk to Score More Than 50 Goals: Al Secord

The Blackhawks began the 1980-81 season with a number of changes, Stan Mikita, Cliff Koroll, JP Bordeleau and Keith Magnuson all retired. General manager Bob Pulford named Magnuson coach. Murray Bannerman was picked up as a backup goalie to Tony Esposito. The team's first-round draft choice, Denis Savard—a Montreal native who didn't speak a lot of English—made the team, along with a 10th-round pick from 1978, Darryl Sutter, who played eight games at the end of the 1980 season.

The Hawks were struggling in mid-December when GM Pulford traded Chicago-born Mike O'Connell to Boston for

Dennis Hull

feisty left wing Al Secord, who had been spending too much time in the penalty box for Bruins management.

Secord joined the Hawks on December 20 in Toronto, and the team responded with a 5-2 victory. Secord played in 41 games and had 13 goals plus 145 penalty minutes, which placed him second on the team.

The next season, Secord led the team in goals with 44 and in penalty minutes with 303, which broke Keith Magnuson's team record of 291. After 59 games, Magnuson stepped down as coach, and GM Pulford took over until the end of the season. Pulford named Orval Tessier the new coach for the '82-83 season. Tessier had coached the Hawk farm team in New Brunswick to the American Hockey League championship. Tessier brought up rookies Steve Larmer, Steve Ludzik, Troy Murray and defenseman Jack O'Callahan from the 1980 U.S. Olympic Champions.

Secord was put on a line with Savard and Larmer and they produced the highest-scoring trio in team history—297 points—breaking the M-P-H mark of 272 set 10 years earlier. Savard broke his own team record of 119 points with 121 on 35 goals and 86 assists. Larmer tallied 43 goals and 47 assists for 90 points to earn the Calder Trophy for rookie of the year honors. Secord became the second Hawk player to score 50-plus goals when he wound up with 54 and 32 assists for 86 points.

Al, now a commercial pilot, told me that he must have had at least a half dozen other shots that hit the goal posts during the season, but was happy he didn't break Hull's 58-goal record. "I had an unbelieveable season. Savvy, Steve and I were all in sync. We didn't have to talk a lot, we just seemed to

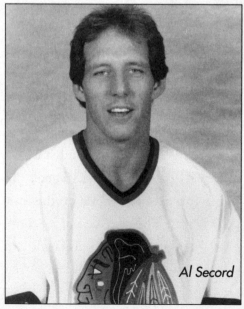

Al Secord

know what each of us were thinking, and it was great!"

Al played for eight seasons for the Hawks, getting 213 goals. He had two, four goal games, both against Toronto at the stadium. Al did it in a November 1, 1981 victory, a 9-4 score, and repeated it January 7, 1987 in a 6-4 decision. In that '87 game, Al scored the goals in eight minutes, 24 seconds, which is still a team record for the fastest four by a Hawk.

Battling Al and Scoring

In his early days with Boston, Secord clashed with Toronto defenseman Dave Hutchison several times. When Al came to Chicago, he was happy to have Dave as a teammate. Al told me that he and Dave used to box to sharpen their skills in a training room at the stadium.

Al racked up 1,426 penalty minutes in his 446 games for the Hawks. Hutchison had 1,550 minutes in the penalty box during his career, with 443 of those coming in his 163 games for Chicago.

Al's first coach in the NHL was Don Cherry, and Al's hometown was Sudbury near Toronto.

As a rookie for the Bruins, Al's family wanted to see him play on his first trip to Maple Leaf Gardens. Al told them he didn't expect to see much ice time. Coach Cherry didn't like his players wearing helmets in those days. Cherry told Al if he played without his helmet he would play him more in the game. Cherry kept his word, and naturally Al's first big NHL fight came against Dave Hutchison of the Leafs!

Stadium Thrills and Practice Shots

Recalling playing in the Chicago Stadium, Al said, "The fans were unbelievable, the noise was deafening, there was nothing like it in the league!"

Unlike the days of the late '60s and '70s when the fun loving Pat Stapleton, Dennis Hull, and Doug Jarrett were pulling their series of jokes, pranks and comedy routines, Al remembers a couple of incidents.

Ken Yaremchuk was a speedy winger who was Chicago's first-round draft pick in 1982. Ken seemed to get on some of his teammates' nerves, especially during practices.

Goalie Tony Esposito told me that whenever Ken went to shoot at practice, he would get out of the net because he never knew where the shot was going to go. Al said that at the end of one practice, defenseman Behn Wilson was already going downstairs to the locker room and had one skate off the ice when Yaremchuk's shot hit his ankle. Wilson was big and tough. He turned around and saw Ken laughing. Wilson was limping and he started chasing Ken around the rink. It took a while for Behn to catch the speedster. When he finally did, he grabbed Ken's stick and threw it up in the empty Stadium seats. Ken responded, "Way to go, Behn!"

A New Drink

Denis Savard was determined to make the Hawks in his rookie season after being a number-one draft pick in 1980. The Montreal native was not fluent in English. After a game, many of the players would usually go out for some liquid refreshment. Savvy was trying to be cool when he ordered a drink in a noisy spot. He asked the waiter for a "Scooby Doo." The waiter asked him to repeat his order. Savvy said, "Scooby Doo." The waiter finally figured out he wanted a "screwdriver."

Although Al had the reputation of being a fighter and a tough guy, hockey players probably take more physical punishment than any other team sport.

In a game in St. Louis, Doug Wilson, who holds the team record for career goals by a defenseman, boomed a shot that went off Secord's glove into Steve Larmer's mouth, pushing his teeth in. Nothing seemed to stop Larmer, who holds the Chicago record for consecutive games played—884— which ranks as third best in NHL history!

Chicago's Winningest Coach: Billy Reay

The familiar fedora patroled behind the Blackhawk bench for 14 seasons, 1,012 regular-season games, 117 playoff games with 573 wins, and 161 ties, which is more than the next three Chicago coaches combined (Bob Pulford, 182; Rudy Pilous, 162; Mike Keenan, 153).

Hawk teams coached under Billy Reay never had a losing record and made the playoffs in all but one season (1968-69), and reached the Stanley Cup finals in '65, '71 and '73. Under Reay, the Hawks had six first-place finishes, three second-place finishes, three third-place finishes and one fourth-place finish.

The lone coaching goal that eluded his career was the Stanley Cup championship. Billy and his players on that '71 team still think about the fateful seventh game when Montreal came from behind to take the cup.

Billy ranks among the all-time leaders in games coached, wins and playoff appearances. His former players all speak highly of him and the way he treated them. The NHL's all-time winning coach with nine Stanley Cups in 30 seasons, Scotty Bowman, told me that Billy was respected for his knowledge of the game, and his players were always prepared.

Billy Played on Two Cup Winners in Montreal

Billy played 10 seasons in the NHL, two with Detroit and eight in Montreal, where he played on two Stanley Cup winners. I saw him in my first Hawk game during the 1946 playoffs when he was playing with the Rocket Richard.

He was regarded as a great psychologist as a coach. Billy told me he developed that approach from the legendary Montreal coach, Dick Irvin. That's the same Irvin who was the Hawks' first captain in their initial NHL season in 1926-27, won a cup for Toronto and three for Montreal in 27 years plus coaching the Hawks in 1955-56.

Reay coached four of the five Hawk players who have their jerseys retired, Mikita, Bobby Hull, Glenn Hall and Tony Esposito, plus All-Star and Hall of Famer Pierre Pilote.

First-Place Finish Finally Reached

Billy regards Chicago's first-place finish in 1966-67 as one of his greatest thrills, since it came in the last season of a six-team league. Also, going from last place, despite a winning record in '68-69, to first place in '69-70 with a half-dozen rookies including goalie Tony Esposito, was a huge accomplishment.

Billy told me, "The Chicago Stadium was great because of the emotion and enthusiasm of the fans!"

"I was fortunate to have great goal keeping in Glenn Hall and then Tony Esposito. When Tony broke in as a rookie in '69-70, he was unbelievable in getting 15 shutouts—something that no one has broken since, and I doubt will ever be broken."

Reay Recalls Hawks Greats

"Bobby Hull had the ability to bring the fans to their feet when he started up the ice while shaking off defenders. Stan (Mikita) had a sixth sense about his play with or without the puck and was really great in setting up his linemates or scoring."

Billy called Dennis Hull and Doug Jarrett Chicago's "Gold Dust Twins." "They were always keeping everyone loose with their jokes and routines."

Jarrett played 11 seasons on defense with the Hawks (1964-75) and was given the title of "chairman of the boards" the way he dished out checks to opposing forwards.

Billy recalls the other comedian of the team for eight seasons: Pat "Whitey" Stapleton. After playing two seasons in Boston, the five-foot-eight defenseman had been sent to the minors after being deemed too small for the NHL. GM Ivan picked up Stapleton in the inter-league draft off Toronto's player list. Stapleton went on to be selected for the NHL All-Star three times ('66, '71 and '72), was named to the 75th Blackhawk anniversary team, and is still tied for the NHL record of six assists by a defenseman in one period (March 30, 1969) against Detroit. Also, the versatile Stapleton, played center in his last year in Chicago ('72-73).

The veteran coach called Keith Magnuson, "A player who always gave you everything he had with heart and determination."

In the two seasons I traveled with the Hawks when I was broadcasting on WLS-FM ('65-66, '66-67), I used to sit next to the coach and trainer Nick Garen on the flights while the players sat in the back of the plane, hiding their beers. I asked Billy, since he was player, whether he knew about the beers. "Sure, Harvey, I knew it was your job to keep me distracted while the players were getting their refreshments!"

Billy usually attended most Hawk home games up to the 2002-03 season when his health and winter weather made it too difficult.

Chicago's First Coaching Change
in 14 Seasons

The Late owner Arthur Wirtz, his son and team president William Wirtz, and GM Tommy Ivan told me one of their most difficult decisions came in December 1976.

The Hawks had won the Smythe Division title the season before, which was Reay's 13th as coach, but were swept by Montreal in the playoffs. Chicago had surprised the hockey world in the summer by signing free-agency All-Star defenseman Bobby Orr. He was the most dominant player in the NHL after Bobby Hull had jumped to the new WHA, but Boston declined to offer him a contract because of his bad knees.

It was evident that Orr was playing in a lot of pain, and even though he could not perform with his previous brillance, he was still above most other defensemen. Orr played 20 games, and the team was 9-9-2 until he was forced to sit out the rest of the season. After he left the lineup, the Hawks' fortunes went south as Tommy Ivan and Mr. Wirtz suggested to Billy Reay that Orr could help him by serving as an assistant coach, which Billy resisted.

The Hawks went 1-12-3 in the next 16 games, winless in 11 (0-8-3) when the "infamous" note was slipped under the door of the coach's apartment a few days before Christmas, relieving him of his duties. GM Ivan named defenseman Bill White interim coach for the rest of the season. White, an All-Star defenseman, had been sidelined with back problems since the previous year. White guided the Hawks to third place, but again they were ousted in the opening round of the playoffs by the Islanders.

Bob Pulford Ushers In New Era for the Blackhawks 1977-78

GM Tommy Ivan told me that for years he had tried to acquire Bob Pulford when he played for Toronto and then Los Angeles, but he was never able to pull off a deal. "Pully" was a hard-nosed two-way center who played on four Stanley Cup championship teams with Toronto. Named to the Hockey Hall of Fame, Pulford scored 281 career goals with the Maple Leafs and Los Angeles. He was captain of the L.A. Kings for two seasons, and when he retired in 1972, he was named coach of the Kings for five seasons. His '74-75 L.A. team still holds the franchise record for most points (105) and fewest losses (17), and Pulford was named Coach of the Year. He repeated that honor in Chicago in 1977-78 when he coached the Hawks to first place.

The only time the Hawks have ever faced Los Angeles in the playoffs occurred in 1974 when Pulford's L.A. Kings were beaten in five games as Tony Esposito had two (1-0) shutouts and allowed only one goal in the other two victories.

In Pulford's second season in Toronto, he was coached by Billy Reay for two

Bob Pulford

years, and it is a little ironic that Reay was basically the coach he replaced when he came to Chicago since Bill White was just an interim replacement. Also, Pully's first NHL goal came against Hawk goalie Al Rollins at Maple Leaf Garden in 1956.

Ivan Names Pulford Team USA Coach, Prelude to the Hawks

Ivan was GM for Team USA in 1976 when he named Pulford to coach the U.S. team in the Canada Cup series. Although Team USA did not medal in those games, Ivan liked the way Pulford handled the squad. With 50 years in almost every phase of hockey, Ivan wanted to step aside to take a less active role with the Hawks. He named Pulford coach and general manager for the 1977-78 season.

With competition from the World Hockey Association, escalating salaries and an aging team, Pulford started to make some deals to reshape the Hawks and bring in some fresh blood.

Dick Redmond was sent to St. Louis for winger Pierre Plante; Pit Martin to Vancouver; Dennis Hull went to Detroit, and first-round draft pick Doug Wilson made the team. Pulford wanted to tighten defensive play, since the year before when the Hawks finished third, they gave up a team-record 298 goals against. Bob "Battleship" Kelly was acquired from Pittsburgh to add some muscle, and rookie Ted Bulley came through with 23 goals, and the team's first Chicago-born player, Mike O'Connell, was added at the end of the season.

The Hawks finished first in the Smythe Division, reduced the goals-against by 78 (220 vs. 298), improved by 20 points, but were knocked out by Boston in the opening playoff round.

1978-79: A Major Trade Before Playoffs

Pully knew that to get to the next level, more had to be done. Bobby Orr had sat out the previous year with more knee surgery, and it was hoped he could make a comeback. However, in pain and unable to play the way he wanted to, Orr retired after six games. First-rounder Tim Higgins joined the team in mid-year, John Marks was enjoying his second season at forward after moving from defense, and Reg Kerr earned a spot after being picked up from Cleveland.

On March 13, 1979, Pulford swung an eight-player deal with the Atlanta (now Calgary) Flames.

They acquired high-scoring center Tom Lysiak and four defensemen: Greg Fox, Pat Ribble, Harold Phillipoff and Miles Zharko. Ivan Boldirev, Darcy Rota and Phil Russell went to the Flames.

The Hawks were in a winless streak, and it took a few games to get back on track. Chicago finished first in the division again, but were swept by the Islanders, who would begin a run of four Stanley Cups the following year.

1979-80: Pulford Steps Back from Coaching

With Hartford, Edmonton, Winnipeg and Quebec joining the NHL, Pulford needed more time to concentrate on being general manager, so he named goalie Ed Johnston as coach, although Pully returned on several more occasions in the '80s and '90s to step behind the Hawks' bench.

Terry Ruskowski and Rich Preston were picked up from the WHA, Ron Sedlbauer was obtained from Vancouver, first and second-round draft picks Keith Brown and Tim Trimper came on board, and defenseman Dave Hutchison was added from Toronto. Injuries ended Keith Magnuson's playing career after three games, and he became assistant coach, and Stan Mikita played only 17 games in his 22nd season before announcing his retirement.

The Hawks finished first in the Smythe Division for the third straight year. In the playoffs, the Hawks swept St. Louis in the first round but fell in four straight to Adams Division champs, Buffalo.

1980-81: Major Turning Point

Pully told me that the drafting of Doug Wilson in his first year as GM and coach was a major step in getting the Hawks back on track, but little did he know that 1980 was even bigger.

Pulford decided to name the popular Magnuson as

head coach as Johnston left to take the post at Pittsburgh. Improved scouting and better drafting were beginning to pay off. Although the Hawks finished first in their division, which usually means not getting a high draft pick, Chicago got two major breaks in the '80 draft. When Quebec joined the NHL the season before, they had Real Cloutier, who was the Hawks' number-one choice in 1976. Under the merger terms, either Cloutier had to come to Chicago, or the Hawks would get a first-round pick in 1979 or 1980. In 1979 Quebec joined the league and wanted to keep its first-round pick to get future hall of famer Michel Goulet. Quebec finished last in its division in 1980 and they wanted to keep Cloutier which meant the Hawks would get the number-three pick plus number 15 in the first round.

That draft saw Montreal take Doug Wickenheiser first, and Winnipeg, needing defense, took Dave Babyich second. Pulford then grabbed Montreal native Denis Savard...enough said!

A 10th rounder from 1978, Darryl Sutter made the team and scored 40 goals. Jerome Dupont was the other first rounder; Steve Ludzik, second round; Troy Murray, third round; and sixth round, Steve Larmer.

Goalie Murray Bannerman had been picked up from Vancouver to complete the Pit Martin deal, and he made the team after spending two seasons with the Hawks' minor league New Brunswick squad.

St. Louis recorded its best season ever with 107 points, while the Hawks finished two games under .500 to wind up second in the Smythe Division. In the playoffs, Calgary swept the Hawks.

Savard, Wilson Set Records; Pulford Returns to Coaching

The NHL realigned the divisions to start the season with the Hawks moving into the Norris Division which now added Detroit, Toronto, and Minnesota besides St. Louis and Winnipeg.

Savard was starting his second season after finishing behind Tom Lysiak in team scoring.

Savard set a team record with 119 points on 32 goals and 87 assists. Doug Wilson fired in 39 goals for another Hawk record and the Norris Trophy as top NHL defenseman.

Al Secord scored a career-high 44 goals, but despite having seven players with 20 goals and more, the Hawks finished fourth.

However, the stress of coaching took its toll on Magnuson, who stepped down after 59 games and Pulford took over.

Chicago took on first-place Minnesota in the playoffs and shocked the North Stars in the series. Next was third-place St. Louis, and the Hawks knocked them off in six games with the final game a 2-0 shutout by Tony Esposito. It was his sixth and last playoff shutout, which stands as a team mark. In the conference finals, Vancouver beat the Hawks in five games.

Rookies, Records and Orval Tessier

With a strong playoff, Bob Pulford returned to his GM duties and named Orval Tessier the new Hawk coach. Tessier had guided New Brunswick to the American Hockey League

Troy Murray

championship. Tessier brought up rookies Steve Larmer, Steve Ludzik and Troy Murray—all draft choices from 1980—plus Jack O'Callahan who played on the 1980 Gold Medal U.S. Olympic Team. Doug Crossman was entering his second full season.

The Hawks responded by taking first in the Norris Division with 104 points—a 32-point jump! Chicago scored a team-record 338 goals. Savard, Larmer and Secord set a record of 297 points by a Hawk line, breaking the 10-year-old mark of 272 set by Martin, Pappin and Dennis Hull; Secord hit 54 goals, and Larmer was named rookie of the year with 90 points, while Savard broke his team mark with 121 points.

The Hawks repeated their playoff run of the previous year. They knocked St. Louis out in four games and did the same to Minnesota in five games. In the conference finals, they had to face Wayne Gretzky and Smythe Division winners Edmonton. The Oilers had finished two points more than the Hawks to get home ice. Gretzky had an "off" season with only 71 goals and 125 assists compared to his 92 goals and 120 assists the year before. Edmonton outgunned the Hawks in four straight, but the Islanders did the same to the Oilers for their fourth Stanley Cup in a row.

Injuries and Suspensions Disappointment!

GM Pulford knew that the Hawks had to add some toughness to go further in the playoffs, so he got defenseman Behn Wilson from Philadelphia in exchange for offensive-minded Doug Crossman. The Hawks had drafted Bruce Cassidy number one in June, and he was regarded as another Doug Wilson, but a freak accident caused a knee injury that limited his NHL career to 36 games in seven seasons.

Secord, coming off a 54-goal season, tore some abdominal muscles and played only 14 games before coming back for the playoffs. His goal total was four. Center Tom Lysiak was slapped with a 20-game suspension when he tripped a linesman in October. Veteran goalie Tony Esposito played only 18 games as Murray Bannerman took over as number one. The Hawks finished fourth and had to face first-place Minnesota. The North Stars avenged two previous playoff losses by taking the best-of-five series 3-2.

Hawks Draft Ed Olczyk, Trent Yawney, and Pulford Coaches Again

Pulford swung a few deals before the draft to assure getting Chicagoan Ed Olczyk as the number-one pick and took defenseman Trent Yawney in the third round. Olczyk joined the team for the season, but Yawney went to the Canadian National team and didn't join the Hawks until 1987. Tony Esposito retired, and Secord did not regain the form he had before his abdominal injury. The team wasn't responding to Tessier, and after 53 games, Pulford once again took over and guided the Hawks to second place. The Hawks responded in the playoffs by sweeping Detroit to face Minnesota again. Chicago had a 2-1 game lead, and the fourth game went into overtime when Darryl Sutter scored for a 7-6 win going back to the Stadium. It was the North Stars' turn to win in overtime 5-4, going back to Minnesota. Sutter was the hero again in the 6-5 overtime decision as the Hawks moved on to Edmonton. The teams split the first four games, but the Oiler offense exploded to win the last two and move on to their second straight Stanley Cup.

Pully stayed on for two more seasons behind the bench and getting the Hawks back into first place in 1985-86.

The First of the Sutters: Player, Assistant Coach and Coach

So far, there has been only one case in NHL history of six brothers playing in the league at the same time. The Sutters —Brian, Duane, Brent, Rich, Ron and Darryl—have combined for a total of 1,320 regular season goals.

Darryl played the fewest seasons (eight) because of injuries, but he made his mark with the Hawks. Drafted in the 10th round in 1978, Darryl spent two years on the Hawk farm team in New Brunswick, and after getting 35 goals was brought up for eight games in 1980 when he scored two goals. He scored 40 goals with the Hawks in his rookie season ('80-81). He had five seasons of 20-plus goals and became team captain in '82-83.

Darryl Becomes Coach

After his playing career was cut short, he became assistant coach and then coached the farm team in Saginaw and Indianapolis, where he won the Turner Cup championship. He returned to Chicago as associate coach to Mike Keenan before becoming head coach for three seasons in '92-93 and guiding the Hawks to the conference finals in 1995.

Darryl stepped down to devote time to his family. He resumed coaching in 1997 at San Jose for five-plus seasons and now has taken over as general manager and coach in Calgary.

Darryl shares two Hawk playoff records: most goals in a playoff year (12) and two overtime goals in one series. Both records were set in 1985.

Darryl scored his first NHL goal against Rogie Vachon in Detroit in 1980. His brother, Brian, played for St. Louis and now coaches the Hawks. Darryl told me that he remembers in one heated game at the Stadium that as Brian and the Blues were leaving the ice, some fans threw a row of seats at them.

Players had certain superstitions, especially when they were on unbeaten strings or scoring streaks. Darryl said at the Chicago Stadium he would only step on the black tiles on the floor, not the white ones.

After Darryl quit playing, he was assistant coach when Duane joined the Hawks. Then he was coach when brothers Brent and Rich played for Chicago. Darryl stepped down as coach to devote more time to his family. He resumed coaching at San Jose in 1997 then moved on to Calgary as GM and coach during the 2002-03 season before resigning in 2010. He became coach of the Los Angeles Kings a year later.

Competing
Against Brothers

Darryl roomed with Rich Preston before he got married. They used to drive in from the suburbs with Steve Larmer and Steve Ludzik. Darryl recalled that both Steves had played together in the juniors and in the AHL before joining the Hawks; however, as they drove together, Darryl said the two would spend most of their time arguing about everything but hockey. It never affected their play.

Despite the heated rivalry with St. Louis, Darryl said when he was on the ice against his brother Brian, he was just another opponent, although the two never got into a fight on the ice, and it was the same when they were coaching against each other. Darryl remembers meeting Billy Reay at his first training camp and being impressed. He calls Bob Pulford an excellent strategist and goalie Tony Esposito a great competitor.

Brian Sutter

Brother Brian Now
Heads Hawks

Brian Sutter took over as Hawk coach in 2001-02 and guided the team back into the playoffs for the first time in five seasons. Brian played for the rival St. Louis Blue for 12 years; served as captain and then coached them for four campaigns; took over at Boston for three and other three in Calgary before Chicago. He was behind the Hawk bench for another three before the 2004-05 season was cancelled.

Brian considers coming to help rebuild Hawks as the "ultimate challenge."

"Coming here is special! It is a great sporting town, and I always enjoyed playing in the stadium because the building and the crowd used to get your adrenaline flowing. I came here because of what the Hawks stand for, and I hope to keep the team competitive."

One thing is for sure, any team that faces a "Sutter coached team" better be ready to compete, especially when the brothers face off against each other. There's only brotherly love when they are not playing against each other!

Trent Yawney Takes Over

The Hawks have been fortunate to have leaders among the draft picks and former players who have turned into NHL coaches and general managers. Before the draft days which started in 1963, Hawk players that eventually went on to become NHL head coaches include such names as Dick Irvin, John Gottselig, Sid Abel, Charlie Conacher, plus recent names like Darryl Sutter, Eddie Olczyk, Dirk Graham, Denis Savard, Duane Sutter, Steve Ludvik, Curt Fraser, and Keith Magnuson to mention a few. Trent Yawney was a third round draft pick in 1984 and coached Chicago's AHL Norfolk team for your years after being Chicago assistant coach. He then coached the Hawks in 2005-06 before being let go 21 games into the following season. Norris Trophy winner Duncan Keith credits Trent with a lot of his development. Yawney demonstrated strong leadership in his career. While drafted in 1984, he didn't join the Hawks until March 1987. He was playing with the Canadian National Team and served as Captain.

Trent told me that he vividly remembers his first NHL game as he joined the Hawks on the road to Minnesota. Bob Pulford had taken over as coach and he assigned to rookie to room with veteran defenseman Bob McGill.

Trent said when he entered the hotel room, McGill was doing push-ups which was fine until the burly defenseman got up to shake his hand—he was buck naked!

Defense Leader: Bob Murray

Like Stan Mikita, Bob Murray played all of his NHL seasons (15) in a Blackhawk uniform.

Murray was a third-round draft pick in 1974 and broke in with the Hawks in 1975 and continued until 1990. He holds the team record for games played by a defenseman (1,008), which ranks fourth behind Mikita, Bobby Hull and Nesterenko. He is second in all-time points by a defenseman behind Doug Wilson. He also served as team captain in the mid-80s.

After his playing career ended, he continued with the Hawks as a scout, director of player personnel, assistant general manager and general manager.

Murray recalled his first NHL goal, which came in Kansas

City on October 25, 1975. It came on a pass from Stan Mikita in a 4-0 win. It was his only goal of his rookie season. The Kansas City franchise moved to Colorado and then on to New Jersey, where it has won three Stanley Cups, the latest in 2003.

Short Goalies, but Tall in Heart!

Bob recalls that when goalie Mike Veisor was called up from the Dallas farm team and GM Tommy Ivan saw him in the locker room for the first time, he said, "We don't need any more stick boys."

Veisor was five-foot-nine and a third-round draft pick in 1972. He appeared in 62 games over five seasons, backing up Tony Esposito and registering three shutouts.

The durable Murray said that Buffalo's Gil Perrault was the toughest to defend, but that Wayne Gretzky always posed the greatest challenge.

Something Big in a Small Package: Darren Pang

You don't find a lot of NHL goaltenders these days under six feet tall. The shortest I can recall is Darren Pang.

When he was signed as a free agent in 1984, he was listed at five-foot-five, 155 pounds, and I assume that was with his skates on!

Darren appeared in 81 games mainly in 1987-88 and '88-89 and despite his size, he actually beat out Bob Mason for the starting job in his first regular season. Darren currently does a great job as an anaylst on ESPN hockey. His career was cut short in a freak accident in practice when teammate Wayne Van Dorf (six-foot-five, 235 pounds) fell on him, wrecking his knee.

Pang Holds Scoring Record

Darren was a feisty competitor, and although you won't find his name in Hawk team records for goalies in terms of shutouts, lowest goals against, or save percentage, Pang does hold the Chicago mark for most assists by a goalie in a season (six). Panger also holds the rookie record for seven consecutive wins.

NHL Debut

Darren made his NHL debut February 22, 1985 at Minnesota when Warren Skordenski pulled a hamstring, but the Hawks lost 4-1.

Darren spent the next two seasons in the minors before winning the backup slot in 1987. He got his first NHL win at the stadium on October 18, 1987, 6-4 over Winnipeg.

Although the Hawk media guide listed him at 155, Darren told me that when he weighed in after the game, the scale only registered 128 pounds. Darren got to see a lot more action after Mason suffered a broken finger in Montreal in mid-November. He responded with back-to-back victories at the Stadium, 5-4 over Gretzky and Edmonton, plus a 5-2 score over Minnesota.

Darren used to take a lot of kidding about his size. He told me that in one game in Montreal, All-Star defenseman Larry Robinson skated by the Hawk bench and referring to Panger, said, "Where's the other half of your goalie?"

Pang: Top-Drawer Goalie

Chicago carried three goalies during most of the 1988-89 season and on the road, the goalies used to room together, but most hotel rooms usually had only two beds. So, the coach jokingly said, "Panger gets the top drawer of the dresser." He was apparently referring to Pang's top-drawer status.

Tony O: Goalie Supreme

The Montreal Canadiens won their second straight Stanley Cup in 1969 by sweeping the expansion St. Louis Blues for the second year in a row despite brilliant goaltending by Glenn Hall. The Canadiens had an abundance of talent plus three goaltenders: Rogie Vachon, Gump Worsley and Michigan Tech college grad Tony Esposito.

The young Esposito appeared in 13 games, had five wins, two shutouts and a 2.73 goals-against average. Montreal could only protect two goalies, and they opted for Vachon and Worsley.

Hawk GM Tommy Ivan was not happy with Glenn Hall's successor, Denis DeJordy, and backup Dave Dryden plus Jack Norris who was picked up in the "infamous" trade with Boston when Tony's brother Phil had been shipped out.

Since the Hawks finished last in the Eastern Division, they had an early pick in the waiver draft. Ivan claimed Esposito for the waiver price of only $25,000.

Even Ivan didn't know how great Tony O. would become guarding Chicago nets for the next 15 seasons.

From Last to First Plus 15 Shutouts

Coach Billy Reay had four college grads to start the 1969-70 season. Besides Esposito, he had the Denver University boys—Magnuson, Koroll and Jim Wiste. The Hawks lost their first five games before tying the Rangers in New York 1-1 on Koroll's first NHL goal. That set the stage for the October 25 game at the Forum against Montreal.

Coach Reay decided to start his rookie goalie against his former team that he won a Stanley Cup with the season before. Esposito was outstanding as he registered his first Hawk shutout in the 5-0 triumph.

Tony went on to record 14 more shutouts to set a modern-day NHL record, which still stands as he won 38 games to set a team mark. Tony's 2.17 goals-against average with the 15 shutouts spearheaded Chicago's leap from last to first, and the Hawks began a string of 28 straight playoff appearances.

Esposito's play put DeJordy on the trading block to Los Angeles. Tony O. won Rookie of the Year honors, top goal tender honors (Vezina Trophy) and was a first-team All-Star. He was named to the All-Star team five times and shared the Vezina Trophy two more times.

Tony O. Holds Most
Hawk Goalie Marks

Esposito holds the Hawk record for most shutouts, games played, most 30-plus and 20-plus win seasons, minutes played in a season, and is tied for most consecutive wins.

Tony told me that he developed his own style of goaltending from watching two of the all-time greats, Glenn Hall and Terry Sawchuk.

Hall was famous for the "butterfly" style, but Tony added some more of his own ideas coupled with quick reflexes. In the 1971-72 season when the Hawks finished first for the third straight campaign, Tony had a record low goals-against average of 1.77 in 48 games with nine shutouts.

That mark stood for 30 years and was just exceeded by Marty Turco of Dallas in 2002-03 with a 1.73 average.

No Fun Facing Bobby's Shots

As Glenn Hall discovered, it was no fun facing Bobby Hull's 100-plus mile-per-hour shots in practice. Tony was no different. He wanted to save his best for the games. Gerry Desjardins backed Tony up for a couple of seasons from 1970-72. Even though all of the goalies were wearing masks, Tony told me at one practice, Bobby ripped a shot off Desjardin's head. Enough said.

It might have been right afterwards when Gerry was asked to see the team dentist, Pat Pull.

Tony Esposito

Christmas Present: New Contacts

As was the case with goalies, they usually roomed together on the road. Desjardins remembers a west coast swing during Christmas 1970. The Hawks had beaten L.A. on December 23 6-4 and headed for Vancouver for a December 26 game. A lot of players had a little bit of holiday cheer the night before.

Gerry told me Tony woke up late and was having a problem with his contact lens, but it didn't stop him from holding back the Canucks 4-2 as Chicago improved its record to 23-6-5.

WHA Plus Expansion Prevents Esposito and Hawks From Cup in 1973

Tony told me that after the heartbreaking loss to Montreal in the 1971 Cup finals, the Hawks continued to dominate in the West Division. However, the Rangers avenged their ouster in the 1972 playoffs.

Defeats are never easy to take, but when the '72-73 campaign began, Chicago lost a lot more.

Atlanta and the New York Islanders came into the NHL and goalie Gerry Desjardins was taken by the new New York entry. Steeper losses came to the new World Hockey Association. Bobby Hull and Chris Bordeleau went to Winnipeg, Andre Lacroix and Bryan Campbell to Philadelphia. Despite these losses, the Hawks knocked off both the Blues and Rangers in five games each in the playoffs to meet Montreal again in the finals.

Again the Canadiens came out on top in six games. Tony O. felt that if they had some of the players lost to the WHA it would have been a different story.

More NHL Expansion in '74-75: Tony Plays 71 Games!

As Tony indicated, it wasn't bad enough that the WHA had taken players from the Hawks, the NHL added Washington and Kansas City (later Colorado and now New Jersey). It did allow the Hawks to move away from Philadelphia in

Grant Mulvey

the West to the new Smythe Division. Rookie Grant Mulvey made the team at the age of 18, and GM Tommy Ivan got center Ivan Boldirev in a trade with California. The defense was weakened with injuries sidelining Tallon, Magnuson and Bill White for half the season each. Esposito played a team-record 71 games, getting a little help from backups Mike Veisor and Michel Dumas in the nine other games.

The Hawks wound up third in the Smythe behind Vancouver, and St. Louis and had to face Boston in the first round of the playoffs in a best-of-three series. The favored Bruins finished second in the Adams Division and were Cup finalists the year before. Paced by the top two scorers in the league, Bobby Orr and Phil Esposito, they demolished the Hawks in the first game, 8-2, going back to Chicago.

Embarrassed, the Hawks made a game out of it, and the score was tied 3-all going into overtime when Ivan Boldirev gave the Stadium crowd something to cheer about with the game winner at 7:33 as Esposito kept the Hawks in it.

The deciding game was the next night in Boston, and Chicago's unlikely scorer, Keith Magnuson, tallied in the first minute of the game as the Hawks stunned the Bruins 6-4 to take the series. In 68 playoff games, Magnuson scored only three goals. Despite the score, Esposito was the difference. Then the Hawks had to face Adams Division champ Buffalo with their league-leading "French Connection" scoring line: Gilbert Perreault, Rick Martin and Rene Robert. The Hawks could not match the Sabres' fire power and were only able to win the one game at the stadium on Mikita's only career overtime goal as Buffalo took the series 4-1.

Gotta Learn to Tap Dance

Tony remembers on one road trip to the west coast, the late Hall of Fame defenseman Eddie Shore showed up at a Blackhawk practice. Shore was a hard-nosed player who also coached Bill White when he played at Springfield in the American Hockey League. Although Shore never played goal and retired from the NHL in 1940, he called Esposito over to the side to give him some advice. The grizzled Shore told Tony, "If you want to be a good goalie, you have to learn how to tap dance!" Tony didn't take Shore's words to heart but managed 15 seasons in tapping out most pucks shot at him to rank seventh in NHL all-time shutouts!

Tony Salutes Hawk Fans

"Chicago has the best group of diehard Hawk fans. It was always fun playing for them. I always wanted to play for Chicago. I wish we could have won a Cup for them."

Although brotherly love is strong, I asked Tony about playing against Phil. Tony said, "Phil always tried to talk to me during a game to distract me."

The Bruins with Bobby Orr and Esposito plus former Hawks Ken Hodge, John McKenzic, and Fred Stanfield, did get the best of Tony and Chicago in the semifinal of the playoffs in both 1970 and 1974. Tony and his teammates paid them back in the 1975 playoff upset.

Two of the Best Honored in 1988

The Blackhawks honored its two greatest living goalies on November 20, 1988 when they retired Tony Esposito's No. 35 jersey and Glenn Hall's No. 1 jersey. It was that same year that Tony was named to the Hockey Hall of Fame. Hall had been selected in 1975.

I remember that 1988 night at the Stadium with the appreciative Hawk fans chanting, "Tony! Tony! Tony!"

Mr. Goalie: Glenn Hall

While the '70s and early '80s belong to Tony Esposito in goal for the Hawks, it was in the late '50s for 10 seasons that Glenn Hall helped turn things around and help the Hawks to the Stanley Cup in 1961. It was fitting that Chicago's finest living goalies got their jerseys retired the same night in 1988 for the two Hall of Famers.

Glenn started his career in Detroit under then-coach Tommy Ivan and in his first full season (1955-56) won rookie of the year honors. Despite a first- and second-place finish in two seasons, failure to win the Stanley Cup after two previous occasions ('53-54 and '54-55), the now Hawk GM Tommy Ivan swung a trade for Hall.

Biggest Steal Ever!

Looking at all-time Hawk trades, getting two Hall of Fame greats, Hall and Ted Lindsay for Forbes Kennedy, Hank Bassen, Billy Preston and Johnny Wilson has to rank as Chicago's best deal of the 20th century!

While Lindsay played only three seasons and was at the end of his career, he added a winning attitude and helped rookie Stan Mikita understand the meaning of staying out of the penalty box.

From Nowhere to Nine Straight Playoffs and a Stanley Cup

Glenn came from a playoff team to Chicago who hadn't been in the postseason for four years. He replaced beleaguered goalie Al Rollins, who is the only player in NHL history to win the Hart Trophy as most valuable while performing for a last-place team. He did it 1953-54 with six shutouts and 12 wins, seven ties in the 66 games he played.

In the previous season, Rollins got the Hawks into the playoffs for the first time in six years.

Glenn didn't have a lot of defensive help in front of him as the Hawks finished fifth, only two points ahead of last-place Toronto. However, Hall had seven shutouts and a respected 2.89 goals-against average.

In the next nine seasons the Hawks made the playoffs and won the Cup in '61—the first time since 1938.

Sick Humor

There were several things that Glenn didn't like about hockey—reporting to training camp and facing shooters like Bobby Hull in practice. The other thing was that Glenn always got stomach problems before a game. He said, "You have to be a little sick to be a goalie."

I remember the time when owners Jim Norris and Arthur Wirtz surprised him with a new car before a game at the stadium against Montreal to honor his consecutive-game streak. Glenn had to make another trip down to the bathroom. He was so unnerved that night it resulted in one of his poorest performances as the Hawks lost 7-3.

Glenn often said about his pregame ritual, "If I didn't get sick, I wouldn't feel right. I doubt that a player who is relaxed before a game can give a good performance."

The Best Ever?

Glenn is credited with developing the "butterfly" style of goaltending.

Before Glenn, most NHL goalies played a stand-up type of game. When the NHL came out with its Century team, Glenn was ranked second to Terry Sawchuk with Jacques Plante third.

Glenn told me that in Eastern Canada, they rank Plante ahead of him.

Certainly, now Patrick Roy has exceeded Sawchuk's records with a lot of contenders like Martin Brodeur and

Dominik Hasek, to mention a few. I know Glenn is one of the best I ever saw in 50 years.

A better judge would be the all-time NHL coach with the most wins and Stanley Cups: Scotty Bowman. Scotty says on naming all-time NHL greats, you really have to measure them by decades, but he puts Glenn at the top of his list. Glenn finished his career at St. Louis where he was coached by Scotty, who also had Plante.

Certainly, Glenn's consecutive streak of 502 regular-season games plus another 50 games in the playoffs—all without a mask—is a mark that will probably never be broken!

Glenn's Views of Today's Goalies

Glenn feels that in today's game the equipment makes a big difference. He thinks that players are better but not the game. He cited the masks, the catching glove, skates and pads. He calls the "save percentage" to rate goalies "a joke."

Although not in favor of the two goalie system, he feels that as long as a goalie is playing well, he should be left in.

Glenn's Records

In going over Glenn's records, it's hard to say he is not the best ever: 13 straight All-Star Games, 84 shutouts (third in NHL history), 115 playoff appearances, three Vezina Trophies, Conn Smythe Trophy for playoff MVP, Calder Trophy, 906 regular-season games and Hall of Fame honors.

As Scotty Bowman said in comparing all-time goalies, "Glenn wasn't fortunate enough to have the luxury of some of the defenses that Sawchuk enjoyed, which makes Glenn's achievements stand out more."

The Mr. Goalie announcement was initiated by my PA precessor, Bob Foster, when he announced the starting lineups. Unfortunately, NHL president Clarence Campbell ordered the Hawks to stop having Bob announce Glenn that way, but in my book, he is still "Mr. Goalie!"

Tough Act to Follow: "Bann-er-Man!"

Just as Denis Dejordy found out in the late '60s when he replaced All-Star goalie Glenn Hall, Murray Bannerman came to the Hawks as Tony Esposito was winding up his brilliant Hawk career.

Bannerman came to Chicago as part of the Pit Martin trade in November 1977. Murray had played exactly one period of NHL hockey with the Canucks. He spent the next two seasons with the Hawk farm team in the American Hockey League before becoming Esposito's backup in 1980. Each season he appeared in more games, as Tony was given more rest, and he kept improving his record. He ranks fifth among all Hawk netminders in wins in his seven seasons.

He played in 60 games in 1984-85 after Tony's retirement.

Murray told me one of his biggest thrills was his first playoff win on April 7, 1982, in overtime at Minnesota (3-2).

Defenseman Greg Fox scored the game winner as Bannerman played an outstanding game. It was one of the first games in which Hawks play-by-play announcer Pat Foley coined his phrasing, "Bann-er-mann, how does he do it?" Naturally, Pat was referring to the sensational stops that Murray was making.

The Hawks, despite finishing fourth, knocked the first place North Stars out in four games, and then proceeded to take out the third-place St. Louis Blues in six games. Murray appeared in 10 playoff games with a 5-4 record. Chicago was beaten in the conference finals by Vancouver. Bannerman ranks fourth among Hawk goalies in wins and games played but is first in assists with five in the playoff.

The "Almost Next" Number 9: Dale Tallon

With the loss of Bobby Hull to the World Hockey Association, along with a few more solid players, the Hawks were looking for someone to fill Bobby's skates. Dan Maloney was a strong left winger who was a first-round draft choice in 1970, and he made the team while Bobby was still with the Hawks. Maloney wore No. 19 and scored 12 goals while spending 174 minutes in the penalty box, second on the team to Keith Magnuson.

Maloney was sent to the minors for 1971-72, but when Bobby went to Winnipeg the next year, Maloney came back in '72-73. The Hawks tried to play up Maloney as the next Bobby, since they still had brother Dennis who was a 30-plus goal scorer.

Maloney could not live up to the hype and was traded before the end of the season to Los Angeles for veteran Ralph Backstrom. Despite a first place for the fourth season in a row, and knocking off St. Louis in the quarter-finals, Montreal outlasted the Hawks in six games for the Stanley Cup.

On May 14, just four days after the final loss to the Canadiens, GM Tommy Ivan traded goalie Gary Smith and defenseman Jerry Korab to Vancouver for Dale Tallon.

Tallon was the number-one draft choice for Vancouver, second overall to Buffalos Gil Perrault in 1970. As a defenseman, Tallon played in the All-Star games his first two seasons and had a career-high 17 goals in '71-72. However, the Canucks were looking for goalie help and a tougher defenseman to make the deal.

New Number 9
Introduced to the Media

The Blackhawks held a press conference at the Bismarck Hotel to introduce the new No. 9, Dale Tallon. Dale told me he was surprised and said to himself he had no intention of ever putting on that number.

When the '73-74 season started, Dale selected No. 19 which had been worn by Dan Maloney, who also had been touted as the Chicago heir to No. 9, but was traded to L.A. before the end of the previous season. Ralph Backstrom was the player for Maloney, but he and Hawk defenseman Pat

Dale Tallon

Stapleton left the Hawks to play for the WHA rival Chicago Cougars.

Tallon had a solid year with 15 goals and 19 assists.

Tallon Moves from Playing to Broadcast Booth

Dale played five seasons for the Hawks and enjoyed his best season in '75-76 when he had 15 goals and 47 assists for 62 points, just missing the Chicago assist record by defensemen, which at that time was 50 by Pat Stapleton.

Dale finished his playing career in Pittsburgh but came back to join Pat Foley in the broadcast booth as a color anaylst.

Dale said he and some of the Hawks used to kid Keith Magnuson about the fact that Maggie didn't score a lot of goals. Maggie fooled him and even himself during a preseason game against Montreal in New Brunswick when he fired the puck into his own net.

Working with Foley for more than 17 seasons in the broadcast booth has resulted in a few slips of the tongue and bloopers. Dale remembers when Sean Hill of St. Louis took a shot below the belt off a Hawk stick. Pat asked Dale whether the puck hit Hill in the left or right knee. Dale replied, "It hit him in the WEE-KNEE!"

Pat Stapleton Clowns off the Ice, but Shines On

There wasn't a lot of demand for short players in the NHL, but Pat "Whitey" Stapleton proved that good things come in small packages. In his eight seasons with the Hawks

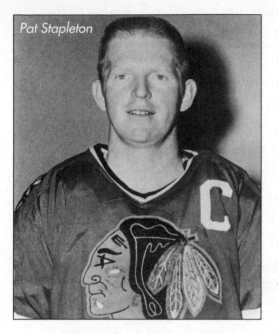

Pat Stapleton

(1965-1973), he set an NHL record for most assists by a defenseman in a season (50); was named to the All-Star team three times and is still tied for the NHL mark with six assists by a blue liner in one period.

After a couple of seasons in Boston, the minors with Toronto, GM Tommy Ivan grabbed him in the waiver draft, which later became the way he landed Tony Esposito. Whitey kept his teammates, opponents and even referees on their toes when he was around. The five-foot-eight, 185 pounder was always pulling tricks.

The Great Race

Whitey's greatest stunt that I witnessed came in 1969 during the playoffs. Johnny Morris, a former wide receiver for the Chicago Bears, was challenged to a foot race by the stocky Stapleton.

The confident Morris indicated that it might be fairer if a faster Hawk like Kenny Wharram, Pit Martin or even Doug Mohns would present a tougher opponent.

Stapleton said no and made a wager with Morris. "I'll race you down the block for a case of beer!" Morris agreed to the bet.

The race was set up on the north side of the stadium (Warren Avenue), and the police set up a lane on the street so the opponents could have a clear path from gate six to Wood Street (east). Betting was picking up, with the newspaper reporters throwing their money on Morris while the Hawk players were backing Stapleton. I remained neutral, but I would estimate that about $1,000 was on the line.

Even though Morris was retired from pro football, he looked to be in good shape. He stripped down to his shorts and was limbering up while Whitey was smiling and talking to his teammates.

The runners were poised, someone shot a starter gun, and they were off! However, Stapleton ran about 15 yards as Morris sprinted down the block. Whitey turned around and strolled back to the starting point. Morris kept going to the end, then came back, puffing and sweating.

Morris asked Whitey, "What's the deal, I beat you, I won!" Whitey replied, "I said I'd race you for a case of beer. I never said I'd beat you!"

Naturally, Whitey and his teammates were laughing while Morris was still puffing from his sprint. The betting money was returned, but I don't know if Johnny Morris ever bought that case of beer.

Missing Typewriter
for Rookie Reporter

Stapleton did not spare anyone from his antics. Bob Verdi was a rookie sports reporter on the Blackhawk beat for the *Chicago Tribune*. On his first west coast road trip with the team, Verdi discovered his typewriter was missing. Verdi was looking all over the arena for the typewriter and was pondering how he would get his story written and sent back to the *Tribune*, not to mention what he would have to do the rest of the road trip.

Somehow, the typewriter showed up just before game time. There's no doubt that No. 12 (Stapleton) was behind it.

Referee Without Skates

I can't remember whether Stapleton was ever suspended, but an incident in Minnesota could have resulted in such action.

As I mentioned, Whitey always had that twinkle in his eye. Veteran referee Bill Friday was set to work the Hawk - North Star game when he looked into his bag to discover his skates were gone after he had stepped out to get a cup of coffee before the game. He called on the trainers of both teams to find him a spare pair of skates in his size. Miraculously, the skates arrived in time, and even though they were not dusted for fingerprints, the handiwork of Chicago's No. 12 was evident.

Stapleton Swings a Trade for Magnuson

The Hawks had four college grads on the 1969-70 team which was probably an NHL record in those days.

Stapleton didn't hesitate to pull a prank on a fellow defenseman whether he had a degree or not. Keith Magnuson played 11 seasons in the NHL—all in a Hawk uniform. Midway in the season, Stapleton pulled Maggie aside and told him that he was walking by GM Tommy Ivan's office when he overheard a conversation that he was going to be traded by the end of the week. Keith was very upset before Whitey told him he was only fooling.

Food Fight?

Whitey didn't pull stunts just by himself. He often enlisted his teammates in the scams.

Showing rookie hockey reporter Bob Verdi that there were no hard feelings after he had hidden his typewriter, Whitey invited the writer to join him for dinner in Vancouver.

Besides Whitey and Verdi, Bill White and Lou Angotti joined them. Everything was pleasant during the meal, and just before the check came, Verdi made an innocent remark. Angotti and White got into a heated argument over the remark and got up in a huff and left. Whitey chastised Verdi for the comment and went after his teammates to smooth things over, leaving the reporter with the check.

When Verdi got back to the hotel, the trio was sitting in the lobby waiting for him and laughing. Bob realized he had been set up again. Oh, yes, the players did split the bill with Verdi, much to the relief of his *Tribune* expense report.

An Astronaut on Ice

Pat Stapleton hails from Sarnia, Ontario, and his son Mike had a few seasons with the Hawks and wore the same No. 12 as his dad.

There's another record breaker from the Sarnia area: Neil Armstrong. He appeared in more NHL games than Gordie Howe and no, he never walked on the moon. This Neil Armstrong is the former NHL linesman who appeared in 1,744 games over 22 seasons from 1957 to 1978.

He was inducted into the Hockey Hall of Fame in 1991.

What does this have to do with Pat Stapleton and the Hawks? Every time Chicago was playing and Neil Armstrong was officiating, Whitey would tell the rookies that linesman Neil Armstrong was the astronaut. Of course, they believed him, because Whitey would never fib!

Chairman of the Boards: Doug Jarrett

Besides the off-ice antics of Pat Stapleton, Doug Jarrett was another comedian along with Dennis Hull when both joined the Hawks for the 1964-65 season.

Doug played for 11 seasons (1964-1975) and ranks fourth among all Hawk defensemen in games played.

Playing with the likes of Pilote, Stapleton, Vasko, Bill White and Magnuson, Jarrett didn't receive much of the headlines. He got the title of "chairman of the boards" for the way he would check opponents.

Doug expressed the highest regard for Coach Reay, but told me the only compliment he remembers from the coach came away from the rink.

On a west coast swing, the team had a few days off and stopped off in Las Vegas. Doug was shooting craps when the coach was passing by and Jarrett was trying to make a "hard six." Jarrett made the point, and the coach remarked, "That's the best play you ever made!"

Flying Too High

I've mentioned several times about how tough GM Tommy Ivan was in contract negotiations.

It didn't matter whether you were Bobby Hull, Stan Mikita or Glenn Hall. Jarrett was coming off a solid year and the team had claimed its first, first-place finish. Doug was doing his own negotiations and asked for $30,000 a year, almost double his salary. The wily Ivan said, "My boy, do you think you're going to be flying in a new 747?" Doug said he was happy to settle for $20,000.

Some Like It Hot!

Coming off the first-place finish in '66-67 and losing players to the new expansion teams, the 1967-68 season got off to a rocky start. The Hawks lost their first six games including ones to new franchises, Pittsburgh and Los Angeles.

Goalie Denis DeJordy, Wharram and Nesterenko were holdouts. Dennis Hull was injured, Chico Maki had an emergency appendectomy, and Doug Mohns had a leg injury. Coach Billy Reay was forced to use backup goalies Dave Dryden and Jack Norris since Glenn Hall was taken by St. Louis in the expansion draft.

In the first four stadium games, New York, Toronto and Boston scored 18 goals and then the new L.A. Kings tallied a 5-3 decision. DeJordy signed, but his first start at the stadium was a disaster: a 7-1 loss to the Bruins paced by former Hawks Fred Stanfield, Ken Hodge and Phil Esposito.

The Hawks began a five-game road trip. They earned a 2-2 tie with the Rangers; got their first win of the season against the new Minnesota team before being clipped in Detroit, 5-1.

With a 1-7-1 record after nine games, Coach Reay was not a happy camper as his team made its first appearance at the L.A. Sports Arena on a hot night (November 2, 1967) against Bob Pulford and the Kings, who beat the Hawks 11 days earlier at the Stadium.

It was a scoreless first period, and the tempers and the temperatures were rising as everyone was grumbling about the heat, which was in the mid-80s.

Reay was not his usual complacent self and in the locker room said, "The next guy that says something about the heat is getting fined!"

Jarrett piped up from the back of the room, "Coach, it's (blank, blank) hot out there!"

Reay snapped back, "What did you say, Jarrett?"

"It's just the way I like it!" Jarrett replied.

The Hawks went out in the second period, and Bobby Hull scored early and set up a Wharram goal as the Hawks won 3-1 to start an eight-game unbeaten string.

Card Tricks, Magic and More

Coach Reay liked to refer to Jarrett and Dennis Hull as the "gold dust twins" because of their routines. They entertained their teammates with jokes, magic tricks and comedy skits, ala Abbott and Costello.

Doug said one of their favorites was imitating a slot machine. They would take turns twisting each other's ears and having a coin pop out of their mouths.

Killing time at the airports, Jarrett, Hull and Stapleton used to attach dollar bills to a string and when people would try to pick them up, they would pull the bills away.

Dick Redmond

The Hawks were gunning for their fourth straight first place finish in 1972-73 despite the loss of Bobby Hull. Tommy

Ivan got defenseman Dick Remond from California in a trade 26 games into the season. The offense-minded Redmond helped quite a bit. Being new to the Hawks meant that Pat Stapleton had a new victim. Whitey waited until the end of December when the team was in Boston. The unsuspecting Redmond discovered his bag was missing when someone came into the terminal calling his name. Stapleton had thrown his bag into the back of a car.

Fastest Three Hawk Playoff Goals

Redmond played five seasons for the Hawks and holds the team record for the fastest two and three goals in the playoffs. Also, he was the first Hawk defenseman ever to get a hat trick in the playoffs, which was later matched by Gary Suter in 1994.

Dick scored two goals 18 seconds apart in the first period at the Stadium on April 4, 1973, against St. Louis in a 7-1 win. His third goal came early in the second period—a span of 7:11. A far cry from the regular-season NHL mark by Blackhawk Bill Mosienko at 21 seconds.

In that same game, Pit Martin had a hat trick; it was the only time two Hawks had three goals each in a playoff game.

Dick had his best season with the team, scoring 22 goals and winding up fourth in team scoring but was traded to St. Louis the next year.

Lou-Lou-Lou

Leaping Lou Angotti had two tours of duty with the Hawks, and whenever he was on the Stadium ice, the fans would chant "Lou! Lou!" In his six seasons (1965-1967 and 1969-1973), the Hawks finished first five times and second once. He was part of history when he assisted on Bobby Hull's record breaking 51st goal against the Rangers at the stadium on March 12, 1966.

Lou told me that his years playing in Chicago were the best of his hockey career. "I had the chance to play with Bobby, Stan, Glenn, Dennis and Pierre."

A lot of Louie's 96 career assists with the Hawks came on Bobby's goals. "Bobby used to tell me, 'Get the puck near my stick, and I'll do the rest.'"

It's Better Than Dental Floss

One time at the Mayfair Bar in Detroit, Angotti told his teammates he could eat broken glass. Then, Lou promptly smashed a glass against the bar and chewed the glass!

Accomplished Musician?

As I mentioned several times, Pat Stapleton never hesitated to try to fool rookies and Hawk newcomers, and he enlisted his teammate Jim Pappin. Playing in the Stadium before the rabid Hawk fans gave the players chills and the opponents fear.

When rookie Dan Maloney joined the team in 1972 at training camp, he heard Al Melgard practicing on the famed Barton organ. Stapleton told Maloney that teammate Pappin could play the organ as well as Melgard.

Stapleton had arranged with the building electrician to have a tape of Melgard's music played over the stadium sound system. Right after practice, Pappin climbed up the east stands to the organ loft at the back of the mezzanine. Pappin sat at the organ and began to play, or at least that's what Maloney thought as the music burst forth.

Maloney was in awe that hockey player Pappin could play the huge organ so well.

Iron Man John Marks

The Blackhawks have been fortunate in getting players from the University of North Dakota. John Marks was a first-round draft pick in 1968, Troy Murray in 1980 and free-agent Eddie Belfour in 1987.

Marks came on board in 1972 and played for 10 seasons, first as a defenseman and later as a winger. John set a team record for playing 509 straight games before a broken leg sidelined him.

His record was clipped by Steve Larmer's 884, which is the third highest in the NHL.

The Hawks opened the 1972 season in Toronto, and it was TV Hockey Night in Canada. Coach Billy Reay made sure that rookie Marks got at least one shift in the game.

Marks was a tough, hard-nosed player and an excellent

fighter, so not too many opponents challenged him. John had two 21-goal seasons when he was switched to wing. John told me that when he played with Mikita, Stan would say to him, "Give me the puck and go to the net."

Ow-Ch-Char!

Ivan Boldirev remembers one incident with John Marks in 1975 in Pittsburgh.

Marks was moving up ice with his head down, when Pittsburgh's Dennis Owchar leveled him with a clean check. Marks was flipped up in the air. Ivan came over to help him up. John looked up and said, "Did anyone catch the license number of that truck?"

Guest Speaker

John was happy when Pat Stapleton invited him to a suburban restaurant for dinner. When John got there, Pat greeted him and told him it was a hockey banquet. After they got inside, Pat told John that he was going to be the guest speaker.

Kidnapped

Since his playing days, John has been in coaching for 20 years. When John was coaching in Kalamazoo, another former Hawk, Phil Russell, played and served as his assistant.

After a practice, a bus pulled up with a bunch of his former Hawk teammates—Mikita, Tallon, Magnuson, and

Koroll. They invited John on board to grab some lunch. John told me before he knew it, they were on their way to Canada for a golf tournament. He had no clothes, golf clubs or a chance to call home. He had fun and didn't file kidnapping charges.

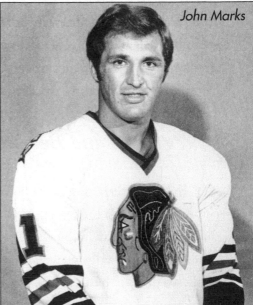

John Marks

Doug Wilson

Thus far in Blackhawk history, there have been three players to win the Norris Trophy—awarded to the best defenseman in the National Hockey League.

Pierre Pilote won it three straight years, a feat accomplished by only two others. Chris Chelios won it twice with the Hawks and once with Montreal. The other Chicago winner is Doug Wilson in 1982.

Doug was a first-round draft pick in Bob Pulford's first year as general manager and coach. Doug was the sixth pick overall in 1977. His first season was solid with 12 goals and 20 assists, but rookie of the year honors went to Willi Plett of Atlanta.

Doug ranks first among all Hawk defenseman in goals, assists and points in addition to being third all time in assists and fifth in points behind Mikita, Hull, Savard and Laramer.

He set a team mark in his Norris Trophy year ('81-82) with 39 goals and 46 assists to finish second to Savard's 119 points. He won All-Star selection three times.

In playoff competition, he ranks fifth among Hawk players in points and assists. He was one of the last Hawk players to play without a helmet, but several head injuries had him using one late in his career.

Pizza and Beer in a Blender

In his banner season of '81-82, Doug Wilson missed four games because of a broken jaw. He took a shot in the mouth that required his jaw to be wired shut. He couldn't have any solid foods and was losing weight from his 185-pound frame. While on the road his team-mates wanted to make sure he got enough nourishment, since he had hardly been able to eat anything. So when they went out in Denver, they asked the waiter to put Doug's pizza and beer in a blender. Doug told me it didn't look pretty, and tasted even nastier! Then, Doug started choking on an anchovy, and they had to break his jaw open.

Doug Wilson

Doug said he thought he would die. Fortunately, he recovered to go on to his record year.

Wedding Party

Players in the late '70s and '80s did a lot together off the ice, and the defensemen were a close knit group. One of the big celebrations was a party to celebrate Tom Lysiak's wedding. It was a hayride and barn dance in the suburbs. Everybody was having a good time, and defenseman Greg Fox wanted to show everyone how good he was in handling horses. Greg stood his ground as the horses galloped toward him, but the six-foot-two, 190 pounder got run over and lost two teeth.

All in all, there was fun for all.

Chris Chelios

The Chicago native finally retired in 2010 after 26 seasons at the age of 48 after being the oldest active player in the NHL. And to think I started doing the public address announcing at the Chicago Stadium before he was born. I am sure Hall of Fame honors aren't too far behind.

Chris started his NHL career in Montreal in 1983 where he became captain, won a Stanley Cup, and a Norris Trophy. Then Chris came back to his hometown in the controversial trade for Denis Savard in 1990 to win two more Norris Trophies with the Hawks. He added two more Stanley Cup ring sin Detroit and was a seven-time NHL All-Star.

Hawk fans also voted him to their 75th Anniversary all-time team for his nine campaigns in Chicago. Chris owns the Hawk records for most assists by a defenseman (58) in a season, which he accomplished twice. In addition he is their all-time leader in penalty minutes, and holds the Hawk playoff record for most goals by a defenseman (six) in a playoff year.

Chelios: First Hawk Defenseman to Lead Team's Scoring

Chris became the first and only Hawk defenseman to lead the team in scoring when he registered 72 points in 1995-96 on 14 goals and 58 assists.

Chelios on the Detroit Trade

Chris told me he hated to leave his home town, especially by being traded to Chicago's archrival, Detroit. "I grew up watching the Hawks, and I always wanted to play for them, but trades are part of the business."

His Red Wing coach Scotty Bowman told me he considered Chris the "fiercest competitor that ever played for him."

Chris Chelios

Chelios Scores Two Overtime Goals and Becomes Captain

Chris tied the team record for most overtime goals in a playoff series in 1995 in Game 3 and 4 in Vancouver as the Hawks swept the Canucks in the conference semifinals. It tied the mark set by Darryl Sutter 10 years earlier against Minnesota, again being set on the road. Chris took over as captain to start the '95-96 season when Dirk Graham retired.

Owners Praised When Winning, Blamed When Losing!

When the team is winning, give the credit to the coach, general manager, players and maybe even the owners, but if you are losing, pass the blame to the coach, GM, players and eventually the owner! Of course, the first one to get fired is the coach—he's the easiest to replace.

To quote the late, great Green Bay Packer coach, Vince Lombardi, "Winning isn't everything, it is the ONLY thing!"

Keith Magnuson said that GM Tommy Ivan told him when he was named coach of the Blackhawks that coaches are hired to be fired.

Most Blackhawk fans starved for a Stanley Cup would probably like to fire its owner—William Wirtz—because in their minds, he's the problem.

I've known the Wirtz family for more than 40 years, and in recent years I have read a lot of stories in the Chicago press criticizing the Wirtz family. They say that he should sell the team, indicating that would be a solution.

I met with Bill and Peter Wirtz extensively for this book. With all the stories written about Bill Wirtz, I am aware of only one sports writer who actually conducted an interview with Bill.

Does Bill Wirtz care about the fans? Does he really want to win the Stanley Cup? Is he willing to spend money to accomplish that goal? Well, I hope to offer some insight and answers to those questions.

First of all, Bill Wirtz is a businessman. In running a business, you want to make money, not lose it! A winning Blackhawk team making the playoffs and being a contender for the Stanley Cup will make money. In recent seasons, the team has seen attendance drop, which translates into losing revenue. This is not a plea for donations.

The Wirtz family bought the Hawks in 1954 and had to make a lot of changes in order to improve the floundering team. Along with the late Jim Norris, it took five years before the Hawks made the playoffs, as the hiring of Tommy Ivan away from Detroit helped turn the franchise around.

Chicago had 10 straight years of making the playoffs, winning the Cup in 1961 and going to the finals again in 1965 plus getting their first, first-place finish in 1967. After finishing out of the playoffs in 1969, the Hawks made the playoffs 28 straight seasons, going to the finals in '71, '73 and '92, plus the conference finals in '83, '85, '89, '90, and '95. The Hawks finished first 13 times in regular-season play since 1970.

Among the original six NHL teams, the New York Rangers have won one Cup since 1940 ('94); Toronto's last Cup was in 1967; and Boston hasn't prevailed since 1972.

Despite having one of the biggest payrolls, the Rangers haven't made the playoffs for six straight seasons. Also, St. Louis ranks in the top five in salaries, and has not won a Cup in 36 years, while Buffalo has been blanked for 33 seasons.

The Chicago area ranks third in population, which would place it sixth behind the three New York-area teams and the two Los Angeles-area squads. Going into the 2002-03 season, the Hawks were ranked 11th in payroll among the 30 teams. Two teams were in bankruptcy, Ottawa and Buffalo.

Bill Wirtz told me that two-thirds of the NHL teams, including the Hawks, lost money in the 2002-03 season. With a potential strike looming for 2004-05, the need for an agreement with the owners and players' association is crucial.

If a strike/lockout occurs, some franchises may fold, which a number of media have indicated might be a good thing.

Hawk Ticket Prices Too High? How About a $30 Per Ticket Raise?

Would you be surprised if I told you that Bill Wirtz thinks the ticket prices are too high?

Based on the current payroll and last season's attendance, Bill told me it would take about an increase of $30 per ticket to have the Hawks turn a profit from the average of $45 per seat at the United Center. Is he in favor of that? "No!"

Peter, Bill and Rocky Wirtz

Granted, that does not take into account all the ancillary revenue and expenses, but again if you view hockey as sports entertainment—the Wirtz family is committed to that concept in addition to running the team on a sound business basis.

For those of you who work for a living, run a company or business, the bottom line is that unless you are non-profit or a governmental agency, it is necessary to run an operation at a profit to survive.

Compromise Agreement

Desipite the efforts of the late Hawk owner, Bill Wirtz, and several other owners, they failed to reach a new collective bargaining agreement with the players' association and the 2004-05 season was cancelled after the contract ended in 2004. Wirtz told me he favored a deal that would be equitable and allow NHL teams to be financially healthy to avoid steeper losses than they were at that time.

The Players' Association indicated that they would be prepared to strike rather than accept any salary cap under a new agreement. They eventually accepted one which is now in effect, although that contract is coming up again. In today's economic times, no one win in a strike/lockout situation which turns fans off.

Handshake Hires Tommy Ivan

Jim Norris lured Tommy Ivan away from Detroit where he had coached the Red Wings to six straight first-place finishes and three Stanley Cups. Ivan was looking for a new challenge, and he certainly got one in 1954 when he took the GM post.

In those days, Bill Wirtz was in charge of financial matters and it wasn't until mid-January that Ivan asked about his paycheck. He hadn't been paid for more than six months since there was no contract, just a Jim Norris handshake. Bill had to check with Jim and his father, Arthur, to find out what Tommy was supposed to get.

Tommy Ivan and Billy Reay

Which is Better: United Center or Chicago Stadium?

The United Center or the old Chicago Stadium. Which do you think Bill Wirtz prefers?

"There was nothing like the feeling of the Chicago Stadium. The fans were close to the action, the noise level was terrific. The United Center is great and is more than three times the size of the old Stadium, but I don't think it can ever capture the atmosphere of the Stadium for 65 seasons."

The Bobby Hull Jump

A lot has been written about the 1972 leap by Hawk superstar Bobby Hull to the World Hockey Association's Winnipeg Jets. Money certainly was the key issue. It's hard to pass up a deal that increases your pay from under $200,000 to two million dollars. Although dollars were the core, a lack of communication on both sides weighed heavily. Emotions and pride were also involved. Both parties indicated to me that things could have been handled better, which "might" have affected the results. Would the Hawks have paid Bobby two million dollars? No. Would Bobby have taken less to stay in Chicago? "Probably."

In those days, Bobby Orr was the highest paid player in the NHL with a salary of $250,000. The lack of communication before the other WHA teams pooled money to up the ante to Bobby plus some of Bobby's resentment from his 15-game holdout in 1969 led to the breakup that deprived Hawk fans of the most exciting player of his day!

Bill told me it was a sad day for him and the Hawks to see Bobby leave. The hatchet was buried in December, 1983 when Hull's No. 9 jersey became the second in team history to be retired. The same year Bobby was inducted into the Hockey Hall of Fame.

Many, Many Thrills for Wirtz

Bill regards Bobby's first time to hit 50 goals as one of his all-time thrills, but admits the emotions and feelings at the 1991 All-Star game are right at the top for him.

It was just a few days after the start of the war against Iraq. The stirring singing of the national anthem, the waving of the flags and the cheering of the sellout crowd of 18,000-plus sent chills through all who were there and even to those watching the game on national TV.

"Finishing first for the first time; going from last place to first are also among my favorite memories."

Wirtz Recalls Hawks Greats

When Bill Wirtz took over as Blackhawk president in 1966, he had the opportunity to see many of the future Hawk stars develop in addition to witnissing some historic milestones.

Besides the thrills from Bobby Hull, Bill regards Stan Mikita as the ultimate Blackhawk, who spent all of his 22 seasons in the NHL. "Stan continued to contribute to the community after his playing career with charitable work for hockey youth with hearing impairment."

On goalies Glenn Hall and Tony Esposito: "Hawk fans were fortunate to witness two of the greatest goalies to ever play in the NHL."

The latest Hawk to have his jersey retired is Denis Savard

on March 19, 1998. "Denis was one of the most creative and exciting players ever to skate for Chicago." Savvy is currently an assistant coach for the Hawks.

"Pierre Pilote was the premier defenseman for the Hawks in the '60s. Only Bobby Orr, playing for Boston, surpassed the level set by Pierre in the '70s before knee injuries ended his career." Orr wound up his playing days for the Hawks, but he was limited to only 27 games in two seasons because of the bad knees.

"Keith Magnuson was the best team player. Chris Chelios was a fierce competitor. Goalie Ed Belfour was always competitive."

Also, Wirtz had high praise for Darryl Sutter, Steve Larmer, Doug Wilson, Dirk Graham, Bill White, Pat Stapleton, Al Secord, Trent Yawney, and Troy Murray to mention a few.

Bill calls Mike Keenan, "A world-class coach."

Also, Wirtz commented on the departures of popular players Jeremy Roenick, Tony Amonte, Ed Belfour and Chelios. "You hate to lose players like that who I respect for their talent. However, in today's game, decisions have to be made that are not too popular when sound business judgements are concerned. It really boils down to a two-way street. We are willing to pay what my hockey managers tell me is fair. Players and agents have certain agendas which may not be on the same level we are seeking. We don't believe in negotiating contracts in the media. With our fans, the city and a fair contract, I would hope we can field a team of players who want to compete as Blackhawks!"

Infamous Trade with Boston Should Have Been Different

Bill Wirtz told me that the major trade in May 1967 should not have taken place the way that Tommy Ivan presented to him and his father, Arthur. The Hawks sent Phil Esposito, Ken Hodge and Fred Stanfield to Boston for Pit Martin, Gilles Marotte and goalie Jack Norris.

Wirtz told me that Gerry Cheevers was supposed to be the goalie in the deal. Bruin GM Happ Emms made a last-minute switch, and Ivan went ahead with it since he was eager to get rid of Esposito. Cheevers went on to lead Boston to two Stanley Cups and was elected to the Hall of Fame while Norris played in only 10 games in two seasons.

Ivan and Pulford Built Up to 28 Consecutive Playoff Appearances

Wirtz credits the efforts of his general managers, Ivan and Bob Pulford, for the team's success in the '60s, '70s, '80s and into the '90s. "Tommy turned things around for us and enabled us to become a regular playoff contender, while Pully continued that tradition in difficult times with expansion and escalating payrolls."

Charity Efforts Increased

Although not highly publicized, the Wirtz family has continued to increase their charitable efforts. On a personal basis, he has contributed millions over the years to causes for the treatment of abused children and people with physical disabilities.

Chicago Blackhawk Charities has been a separate entity since 1993 and has contributed nearly five million dollars to underprivileged and abused children, physically disabled individuals, and various youth hockey programs to just mention a few. The Blackhawk Charities are in partnership with the McCormick Tribune Foundation, which provides matching funds and administrative assistance.

The Blackhawk Charities support many youth hockey programs and clinics.

New Urban Hockey Program

Bill Wirtz is proud that the Hawks have undertaken a program to boost urban/inner city hockey. "I hope to see the day when there are more African-American players in the National Hockey League."

Two Hockey Halls of Fame

Bill Wirtz has received many hockey honors which include induction into the Hockey Hall of Fame in 1976 and the U.S. Hockey Hall of Fame in 1985 plus being named recipient of the Lester Patrick Trophy for outstanding service to hockey in the United States.

Despite his many other honors and awards, he told me nothing would make him happier than seeing the Stanley Cup return to the Blackhawks!

Peter Wirtz

The Wirtz organization always made sure that they family members were active in the Chicago Blackhawks when they assumed ownership along with James Norris in 1952. Peter Wirtz served as Vice President and supervised off ice activities until his father dies in 2007. He helped to improve the atmosphere for fans at the United Center.

He recalled to me one of his earliest Blackhawk enterprises as he was growing up watching Bobby Hull, San Mikita, and Tony Esposito. "I made a deal with Bobby to autograph pictures; then I would sell them for a dollar and give him 10 percent of the profits."

"There was a special aura of the Chicago Stadium, and the All-Star Game when the Gulf War broke out, and the crowd response was truly a patriotic moment."

Steve Sullivan and Jocelyn Thibault Extend Charity Efforts

Blackhawk players have always taken an active role in helping Chicago area charities. Many times the spotlight is focused on salaries that professinal athletes are paid and their acts of public serivce and charities don't get the same attention.

During the 2003-04 season, Hawk winger Steve Sullivan and goalie Jocelyn Thibault leased a nited Center skybox to donate 12 tickets to sport youth organizations and other worthy charity groups to attend home games.

Duncan Keith and his wife have set up a charity for Chicago area children and center Dave Bolland has started a foundation to assist youth with community programs in the areas of arts and sports. Former Hawk defenseman Brian Campbell established a program to aid autistic children.

My First Penalty Shot

Getting back to my pure fan days, I remember my first penalty shot. It was New Year's night, January 1, 1952. Montreal's Rocket Richard was tripped up on a breakaway just 12 seconds into the game. The Hawk goalie was veteran Harry Lumley who was picked up in 1950 from Detroit after the Red Wings won the Stanley Cup because he was replaced by Terry Sawchuk. Lumley moved out and the Rocket gave him a head fake as the goalie moved and Richard put it into an open net. The Canadiens won the game 3-0. There wasn't another penalty shot at the Chicago Stadium for 10 more years (January 31, 1962) and it was another year before one was scored (November 20, 1963).

There was a 35-year span at the stadium before a Hawk scored on a penalty shot. Cliff Koroll got one against St. Louis (October 24, 1976) to match the one that Bert Gardiner tallied on December 4, 1941 against Montreal, just three days before the attack on Pearl Harbor.

Montreal's Jacques Plante's Playoff Debut

After seeing my first game as a fan in the 1946 playoffs, the Hawks didn't make it to the postseason for six more years. Chicago was composed of a bunch of veterans near the end of their careers in 1952-53. Fortunately they had gotten goalie Al Rollins from Toronto to sneak into the playoffs, two points ahead of the Maple Leafs. The Hawks faced favored Montreal.

Chicago's roster included Bill Mosienko along with Sid Abel, Jim Peters, Gus Bodnar, Bill Gadsby, George Gee and the team's leading scorer, Jim McFadden. The Hawks had to win their last two games to make it into the postseason.

The Canadiens had home ice and won the first two games 3-1 and 4-3. At the Chicago Stadium, goalie Rollins kept them in the game that went into overtime 1-1. Then, a little more than five minutes in the extra session, defenseman Al Dewsbury, scored to give the Hawks a 2-1 win.

It was the only playoff goal of his NHL career, and he had only five goals all season. In the next game, Chicago evened the series with a 3-1 decision, again thanks to Rollins.

Returning to the Forum in Montreal where the Hawks had won only two games out of seven during the season, Chicago stunned the Canadiens 4-2 to take the series lead 3-2. One more win at the Stadium and the underdogs would be in the finals. Canadien coach Dick Irvin, who was an original Hawk in 1926-27, decided to start rookie Jacques Plante in goal in place of veteran Gerry McNeil. It was Plante's first playoff start.

On the opening faceoff, the Hawks top scorer, Jim McFadden, broke in alone past Doug Harvey and rifled a 25-footer at the goal. Plante kicked it aside which turned out to be Chicago's best shot of the night. Plante notched his first playoff shutout 3-0 and the Canadiens tied the series and returned to Montreal for a 4-1 win. The Canadiens went on to win the Cup.

1959 Playoffs: Stadium Erupts

It took the Blackhawks six more seasons to get back to the playoffs and they had the envious task of facing the Montreal who had won three straight Stanley Cups as the 1959 playoffs got underway. Chicago was on the rise as GM Tommy Ivan had made some trade deals and the team had a farm team in Buffalo plus the St. Catharine's junior team was paying off.

Glenn Hall was in his second season, captain Ed Litzberger was a 33-goal scorer, veterans Ted Lindsay and Tod Sloan provided experience for youngsters Bobby Hull, Elmer Vasko, Ken Wharram, and Pierre Pilote was establishing himself as a top flight defenseman.

Montreal won the first two home games, 4-2 and 5-1, but the Hawks bounced back at the Stadium 4-2 and 3-1 to tie the series. The Canadiens took the next game at the Forum 4-2 to return to Chicago with one more victory needed to move into the finals.

April 4, 1959 was one of the most wild games ever in Chicago. The referee was veteran Red Storey and it was the last game he ever officiated in the NHL. The game see-sawed back and forth, but on three different occasions, Blackhawk players were tripped and hooked. It was bad enough that no penalties were called on those three situations, but all three times the Canadiens got the puck off the non-calls and scored. Montreal won the game 5-4 and the series to move on and win their fourth straight Cup.

Immediately as the game ended, angry fans showered the ice with debris. Several fans raced on the ice, one with a chair and another with a cup of beer to throw at the referee. Montreal defenseman Doug Harvey hit one of the fans with stick before order was restored.

When the press asked NHL president Clarence Campbell about the officiating after the game, Campbell said that apparently Roy "Red" Storey "choked." Without support, Storey resigned the next day. Storey defended his officiating, saying he felt he should let the players play on.

Outside of that blemish on his record and many efforts for him to return, he did not. Storey was voted in the Hockey Hall of Fame in 1967.

Stepping Stone to the Cup: 1960 Playoffs and My Radio Debut

The Canadiens started the 1959-60 season in a quest for a fifth straight cup. From 1942 to 1960, three teams out of the original six, were the only ones to capture the cup— Montreal (eight), Toronto (six) and Detroit (five).

Coach Rudy Pilous added center Bill Hay from college,

Stan Mikita from the juniors and the continued improvement from Bobby Hull, Pierre Pilote and Glenn Hall. The team lost captain Ed Litzenberger in January when coming home from a party. His car crashed killing his wife and leaving him seriously injured. He managed to return before the playoffs.

The Hawks had to overcome a horrendous start that season. They won the opener over the Rangers 5-2, but then went winless in the next 14 (0-11-3). After losing their captain they came on strong to match their previous season point total to wind up third.

The Blackhawks had no radio or TV coverage all season. I was working at WLS Radio doing news and sports. I tried all season to get the games on the radio to no avail. My motive was selfish because I wanted to do the play-by-play. WLS wasn't interested, but WCFL AM 1000 was. All I had to do was get the OK from the Hawks and sponsors to pay for the time.

I kept after GM Tommy Ivan all season. He told me I could get the broadcast rights free if I could get the games on before the playoffs. I couldn't. I sent out dozens of letters to potential advertisers. Finally, Pabst Blue Ribbon beer wanted a letter of first refusal to sponsor the games.

The Hawks clinched third place and were finishing the season in Boston on March 20. I sent Tommy Ivan a telegram at Boston Garden, and he called me that night after the game, saying that owner Jim Norris granted me the rights to broadcast the playoffs. Monday morning I called the advertising director at Pabst, but he then told me that he would only sponsor the games if I could get Pabst beer sold in the stadium.

I called a high school friend (Joe Sigman) who was working at Bud Solk Advertising to see if he could get someone to sponsor the playoffs on WCFL. I went to his office and we started going through the phone book to find a sponsor. The first game was Thursday in Montreal. Late Tuesday afternoon, the president of Republic Savings who was a Hawk season ticket holder agreed to sponsor the games. Then we finalized things with the radio station Wednesday.

I was excited, but then I was told since Harvey Wittenberg was not known, The Hawks public relations director, former player and coach Johnny Gottselig, would do the play-by-play, and I would add the color.

There wasn't enough time for me to get to Montreal for the first game which the Canadiens won 4-3. I made it up for the second game to work with Gottselig. It was the first time that I was in the Montreal Forum. The building just reeked with hockey tradition. The broadcast booth was up in the rafters and you had to look down to the ice and sideboards below. It was an exciting game as the Hawks rallied to tie the game 3-3 and send it into overtime. Gottselig asked me to get a guest to interview before the overtime started. Ranger goalie Gump Worsley and Boston goalie Don Simmons were at the game. Being a rookie announcer, I went up to Worsley. His conversation with Simmons was puncuated with swear words. I said to myself, "Here's a chance to interview an NHL goalie, but if he swears like that, this might be my first and last radio broadcast!" Forunately, Gump behaved and my career was extended.

The overtime began and the Hawks started strong. Seven minutes into the overtime, Bill Hay's shot hit the crossbar and about a minute later, Montreal's Doug Harvey fired a screen shot that beat Glenn Hall to give the Canadiens a 4-3 win.

Montreal came back to Chicago and behind the goaltending of Jacques Plante, blanked the Hawks 4-0 and 2-0 to sweep the series and then move to the finals where they captured their fifth straight Cup.

Although my brief on-air radio hockey career ended, it enabled me to establish myself with the Hawks and GM Tommy Ivan which eventually led me to being the stadium back-up public address announcer and then regular PA announcer for the next 41 seasons in December 1961.

Olympic Hero's NHL Debut Spoiled

The United States performed their first "miracle on ice" by stunning the hockey world with their upset of Russia in the 1960 winter olympics. One of the heroes was goalie Jack McCarten who was property of the New York Rangers. McCarten joined the Rangers on their road trip after the Olympics and they wanted the U.S. goalie to make his NHL debut at Madison Square Garden when they got home to boost their attendance. In those days, teams only had to dress one goalie. Veteran Gump Worsley was the starting goalie when they came to the stadium. McCarten was in the press box and since he wasn't expected to play, he was enjoying the free food during the game. With less than two minutes to go in the second period, Bobby Hull drove to the net and accidentally cut Worsley's hand as he skated across. Worsley couldn't continue and since the period was almost over, the referee sent the players to the dressing rooms to finish the period later. The call came to the press box for McCarten to get dressed to play the rest of the game. McCarten had been stuffing his face during the game, and turned white and then a little green. He went to the locker room and made his debut. Fortunately for the Hawks, he did not repeat his Olympic performance, and gave up three goals as Chicago won the game.

McCarten played two seasons with the Rangers and appeared in only 12 games, but did register his only NHL shutout the following October in New York against the Hawks 2-0, but that didn't stop Chicago from eventually winning the Stanley Cup the following April.

Taking Over as the Stadium Voice of the Blackhawks

I took over as the Chicago Stadium public address announcer on January 1, 1962 and my first game was Glenn Hall's 2-0 shutout over Montreal. In those days, there weren't too many tough names to announce. The only Hawk I had to worry about was Bill Hay who told me never to announce his nickname "Red." He said, "My name is Bill." The French Canadians were easy: Jean was "Jon," Guy was "Ghee," Bonin was "Bonee," Langlois was "Langwah," etc.

The Hawks finished third for the fourth straight season and again defeated Montreal in the semifinal playoff series, 4 to 2, but fell to Toronto four games to two in the finals.

The highlight of the regular season came on the road at New York when Bobby Hull became the third NHL player to score 50 goals in one season, matching Montreal's Rocket Richard and Bernie Geoffrion. The milestone came on the final regular-season game, March 25, 1962. Also, Hull tied New York's Andy Bathgate for the league scoring title with 84 points, but got the nod because he scored 50 to Bathgate's 28 goals.

Another high note came on January 17, 1962 when the Hawks were facing Montreal at the Stadium, and owner Jim Norris surprised goalie Glenn Hall by presenting him with a new car before the game. The car was driven on the ice. Hall, who was always nervous before a game and usually had an upset stomach, turned white. He went back down to the locker room again.

The event really upset him. Early in the opening period, Montreal's Jean Beliveau bounced a shot from center ice that skipped past Hall who had one of his worst nights in a 7-3 loss to the Canadiens. It was Hall's 552 consecutive appearance including playoffs. His streak of consecutive regular-season starts continued to 502 into the following campaign and finally ended against Boston on November 7, 1962.

1965-66: WGN-TV and WLS-FM Broadcast All Road Games

With All-Stars like Hull, Mikita, Hall, Pilote and Ken Wharram, the games at the Chicago Stadium were sold out. At the start of the 1964-65 season when WGN-TV made a new deal to televise Hawk road games, the Hawks told the TV management that unless they did all the road games, they would not be allowed to carry the playoff games. Channel 9 had been doing select road games, mainly on Saturdays. So when the playoffs started, the Hawks took over to show home games on closed-circuit theatre TV and the road games at the stadium. Since the regular play-by-play broadcaster, Lloyd Pettit, worked for WGN, I was asked to work with Bob Elston, who was better known for baseball, but had done some hockey broadcasting in the 1950s.

All-Star Game on FM

I did the road games again next season on WLS-FM up against WGN-TV, and again I had one exclusive Saturday afternoon. Also, I had another first, when I broadcast the All-Star game in Montreal. The Hawks had five players on the team: Hull, Mikita, Pilote, Hall and Wharram.

The All-Star game had always been played at the start of the season with the Stanley Cup champion facing All stars. In 1967, the game was moved to January with Montreal blanking the Stars 3-0. I know it was the first time that a road All-Star game was broadcast in Chicago on FM.

Following the game, the Hawks were on the road to Boston. I was traveling with the Hawk stars on a flight from Montreal via Northeast Airlines. Glenn Hall wasn't wild about flying and especially on this flight when the pilot announced that the plane was experiencing some technical problems and had to fly at only 10,000 feet. This meant a rough flight and I saw Glenn's face turn green and then white. The bumpy ride didn't affect his play in Boston Garden where the Hawks won 4-2.

Ides of March

March 12, 1967 turned out to be another good luck day in Blackhawk history. A year earlier, Hull broke the NHL record with his 51st goal. This proved to be the date when the Hawks clinched first place for the first time in regular-season play to break the "Muldoon Curse." Pete Muldoon coached Chicago in its first year (1926-27) and was fired after a third-place finish. He told the owner, "If you fire me, I'll put a curse on your team so you'll never finish first."

That lasted 40 years.

Strangest Goal Ever at the Chicago Stadium

Any hockey fan who has ever seen many games could probably recall a wierd goal. Just when you thought you'd seen it all, there's something new. Now with video replay, it's a lot easier. Shots that appear to go wide, deflect off sticks, skates, legs, heads, shoulders, and goal posts sometimes find their way into the net. Players and goalies have knocked the puck into their own goals. Goalies have scored the length of the ice into open nets. The human goal judges have missed seeing goals or turned on the goal light without the puck going into the net. I remember broadcasting a game in New York in March 1967 when Bobby Hull was going for his third 50-goal season. His 45-foot slap shot appeared to go in and out of the net in a flash. Referee John Ashley raised his arm indicating a goal, but the goal judge didn't turn on the light and Ashley let the game go on. Bobby wound up with 52 that season. I guess I could go on to mention that fatal shot from center ice in the seventh game of the '71 Cup final or when Glenn Hall got a new car and Montreal's Jean Beliveau bounced a puck past him, again from outside the blue line.

The goal that I found to be the strangest ever at the Chicago Stadium occurred in 1960 against Boston. Veteran linesman Matt Pavelich was promoted to referee that season. Matt was a capable official, who ranks second in all-time games, and worked during the regular season and playoffs.

The Hawks were playing the Bruins. A Boston player fired a shot at the Hawk net that appeared to beat Glenn Hall, but no light went on and the puck was behind the net as the Hawks gained control and moved up ice into the Boston zone. As Pavelich skated past the Bruin bench, their players stood up, yelled and banged their sticks against the boards.

Pavelich whirled around, blew his whistle and called it a Boston goal. Upon inspection, there was a small hole in the Hawk net which accounted why the puck wound up behind the goal. General manager Tommy Ivan told me after the game he had never seen anything like it!

1961: The Third Stanley Cup

Montreal was shooting for their sixth straight Stanley Cup when the '60-61 season got underway. The Canadiens had finished first in four of the past five campaigns and boasted the top two league scorers in Bernie Geoffrion and Jean Beliveau plus Dickie Moore and Henri Richard.

Geoffrion became the second player to score 50 goals in a season, matching that of teammate Rocket Richard who had retired the previous season.

Although the Hawks and Canadiens had split their games during the regular schedule (5-5-4), Montreal was a favorite against Chicago which had finished third. The Canadiens had beaten the Hawks five straight times in the playoffs (1944, 1946, 1953, 1959, 1960). Veteran goalie Jacques Plante had led the NHL in goals against for five straight seasons.

The Hawks still had a fairly young team with Hull, Mikita, Hay, Murray Balfour, plus veteran Hall in goal while Pierre Pilote was establishing himself as a premier defense-man. Other veterans included Ken Wharram, Ab McDonald, Tod Sloan, Ron Murphy, Ed Litzenberger with defensemen Moose Vasko, Al Arbour, Dolly St. Laurent and utility tough guy Reg Fleming.

Montreal had the home ice and won Game 1 6-2. The Hawks shocked the defending champs in Game 2 4-3 on a goal by Litzenberger.

Overtime Delight

Game 3 at the Stadium was one of the most exciting I ever saw. Chicago took a 1-0 lead which lasted until the last 36 seconds of regulation time. I, along with GM Ivan, had left the press box when Montreal pulled goalie Plante for an extra attacker. I was going to phone in my game report to WLS radio when Henri Richard tied the game to send it into sudden death overtime.

The game went into the third overtime and it was almost 2 a.m. when Murray Balfour scored on a power play at 12:12 of the third extra period for the second longest game in Hawk history.

The other was also against Montreal on the road in April 1931 when Cy Wentworth scored for Chicago.

The Canadiens roared back in the fourth game, firing 60 shots at Glenn Hall for a 5-2 win to tie the series 2-2 going back to the Forum.

Chicago was not to be denied and goalie Hall blanked the Canadiens 3-0 in Game 5 and repeated in Game 6, 3-0, to win the series and move to the finals for the first time since 1944 when the Canadiens swept the Hawks. The clinching game came on April 4, which was the two-year anniversary of the controversial loss to Montreal at the Stadium when referee Storey failed to make several penalty calls, touching off a near riot.

Going into the finals, third-place Chicago was facing fourth-place Detroit which had upset second-place Toronto. Chicago had taken the season series 6-4-4, but hadn't faced the Red Wings in the playoffs since the 1944 semifinals when they won. Detroit had Terry Sawchuk in goal and the high scoring line of Gordie Howe, Alex Delvecchio and Norm Ullman.

Playoff Format Altered

Because both cities were close, the playoff format was changed. Instead of each team playing two in a row at home, the games were alternated. The Hawks won the opener 3-2 with Hull getting two goals. Detroit took the second game 3-1. Returning to the stadium, the Hawks won 3-1, but back at the Olympia, the Wings tied the series with a 2-1 decision. Following form, the Hawks roared back at home with a 6-3 victory. The sixth game in Detroit saw the Wings grab a 1-0 lead in the first period, but in the second on a short-handed situation, penalty killer Reggie Fleming got his first goal of the playoffs to tie the game. Chicago took the lead for good when Ab McDonald banged in Hull's rebound shot. The Hawks added three more in the third period for a 5-1 triumph and their first Stanley Cup since 1938.

The players carried goalie Hall on their shoulders. It was a sweet celebration for GM Ivan who left Detroit to build up the Chicago franchise and Hall who was traded to the Hawks because they felt Sawchuk had more potential. Hawk defenseman Pilote tied Howe for the playoff scoring title with 15 points in 12 games.

Close Again but No Cup!

The Hawks came close to repeating in 1962, a year that saw Bobby Hull score his 50th goal on the last game of the season in New York to match the records of Montreal's Rocket Richard and Bernie Geoffrion. The Hawks finished third and faced Montreal in the playoffs for the fourth straight time. Montreal won the first two games, but Chicago took the next four to move into the finals against Toronto. The Leafs had home ice and won the first two. The Hawks tied the series by taking the next two at the stadium. Toronto gained the upper hand in game five with an 8-4 battle and then won the Stanley Cup by edging Chicago 2-1 at the stadium.

The next seasons saw the Hawks finish second, one point behind Toronto which meant they would face fourth-place Detroit in the playoffs. Chicago won the first two at the Stadium, but the Red Wings swept the next four to move into the finals. Two straight playoff defeats cost coach Rudy Pilous his job as Tommy Ivan replaced him with Billy Reay who had played on two Stanley Cup winners in Montreal and had coached Toronto for two seasons. Reay went on to coach the Hawks for 14 seasons with 516 wins and 161 ties in 1,012 games. Reay has more wins than the next three coaches combined (Bob Pulford, Pilous, Mike Keenan) with six first-place finishes and getting his team into the playoffs 13 times.

Unknown Goalie Stymies Hawks

In Reay's first season, the team again missed first place by one point as Mikita and Hull led the NHL in scoring, but again the fourth-place Red Wings edged Chicago in playoffs four games to three. The key game in the series was Game 2 when Detroit goalie Terry Sawchuk got injured in the first period and was replaced by minor leaguer Bob Champoux who appeared in his first playoff game. Champoux faced more than 40 shots, gave up four goals, but the Hawks lost the game 5-4.

It was Champoux's only playoff appearance among the 17 NHL games he played in.

Ivan Trades Veterans

GM Tommy Ivan made some trades to shake things up. Murray Balfour, Ab McDonald and Reggie Fleming were sent to Boston for 31-year-old Doug Mohns and Matt Ravlich. Mohns, a defenseman with speed, was put on a line with Mikita and Wharram. Rookies Fred Stanfield, Doug Jarrett, and Bobby Hull's younger brother Dennis joined the team in '64-65. The Hawks finished third with Mikita winning his second straight scoring title and this time Chicago turned the tables on first-place Detroit by coming from behind to win Games 6 and 7 to move into the finals against Montreal. The series went the full seven games with the home team prevailing in each contest. The Canadien goal tenders, Gump Worsley and Charlie Hodge, came up with three shutouts to thwart the Hawks.

Hull Gets Second 50-Goal Season

In '65-66 when I was doing the play-by-play on WLS FM, the highlight of Bobby Hull becoming the first player to score more than 50 goals in a season twice by getting 54 was great. His record breaking 51st came on March 12, 1966, at the Stadium and I was fortunate to announce it before the sellout crowd. The noise gave everyone, including all the Hawk players, goose bumps. Another thrill for me came on New Year's Eve in Detroit. The Wings were always tough on the Hawks at the Olympia and Coach Reay surprisingly called on backup goalie Dave Dryden to face Detroit instead of Glenn Hall. Dryden was the older brother of Ken who later starred for Montreal. The score was tied 1-1 when Frank Mahovlich had a breakaway on Dryden. Mahovlich wound up his career with 533 goals. Dryden made a key save and the Hawks went on to a 4-1 win and moved into first place. I complimented Dryden after the game and asked how he stayed so cool in making that stop. Dryden told me, "I was too frightened to move and his shot hit me."

In the 1966 playoffs, Detroit knocked off the Hawks four games to two.

Expansion Hits in 1967-68

Coming off their first, first-place finish in the last year of the original six teams to break the 40-year hex of the "Muldoon Curse," expansion to 12 teams took its toll along with the disappointment of the playoffs.

Coach Billy Reay had the task of finding replacements for the loss of Glenn Hall to St. Louis, defenseman Ed Van Impe, spark plug Lou Angotti, Bill Hay decided to re-retire, and Matt Ravlich would miss the season due to a broken leg.

Mikita continued his sparkling play by repeating his unduplicated feat of winning the scoring trophy (Ross), beating out former teammate Esposito, the most valuable (Hart) and the Lady Byng trophy. Bobby Hull had a great season for most (44 goals), but missed five games and another try for his third straight 50-goal campaign. Denis DeJordy did the bulk of the goaltending backed by Dave Dryden.

The Hawks finished fourth behind Boston and faced the second-place Rangers in the playoffs whom many had predicted would win the cup. The New Yorkers had just missed over taking Montreal for first place. Chicago had finished the regular season winless in their last six games and barely made the playoffs ahead of the defending champion Maple Leafs.

Hawks Upset Rangers on "Bobby Who?" Goal

The Rangers with home ice took the first two games at Madison Square Garden and then headed to Chicago. The visitors appeared on their way to make it three in a row by leading the Hawks 3-2 going into the third period. Coach Reay shook up his lines and put Mikita, Hull and Ken Wharram on the same line. The Hawks clicked for five third-period goals and won the game 7-4 and then evened the series in Game 4 3-1 heading back to New York for Game 5.

The game was tied 1-1 with less than four minutes remaining in the third period and appeared headed for overtime when an unlikely hero emerged. Bobby Schmautz had played in 13 games during the regular schedule and scored only three goals. He fired a shot from center ice and headed to the bench. He never saw it go in and fortunately neither did Ranger goalie Ed Giacomin as he lost sight of the puck. That gave the Hawks the edge as they headed back to the Stadium where they took a 4-1 decision and a trip to the finals against Montreal.

The Canadiens had outbattled Boston and had home ice advantage. They swept the first three games in the best of seven, but the Hawks fought back to take the fourth 2-1. Back at the Forum for Game 5, Chicago pushed the Canadiens into overtime and almost won it but Montreal prevailed to move into the finals and sweep St. Louis for their third cup in four years.

1968-69: Best Last-Place Team Ever

For the first time in 10 seasons, the Hawks failed to make the playoffs as they wound up last in the Eastern Division despite a winning record (34-33-9) which would have placed them second in the expansion Western Division.

Bobby Hull scored a record 58 goals, his fourth 50-plus and 107 points, a team mark, but lost the scoring race to former teammate Phil Esposito who had 49 goals and 126 points for Boston. Also, Chicago set a team record 280 goals in 76 games, but allowed a division-high 246 goals against.

Former Hawk Glenn Hall shared the Vezina trophy for goalies with St. Louis teammate Jacques Plante.

The team had five 30-plus goal scorers which is still a Hawk record in one season and two more 20-plus goal scorers. Besides Bobby, Mikita, Wharram, Dennis Hull and Jim Pappin all had 30-plus goals.

Pappin had been picked up in a trade with Toronto for veteran Pierre Pilote. The two other 20-plus scorers were Doug Mohns and Pit Martin. Pat Stapleton set a team record for assists with 50, breaking Pilote's mark. Stapleton got an NHL record tying six assists in one period in the season finale at the Stadium.

From Last to First
with a College Education!

There's no doubt that changes had to be made if the Hawks were to return to the playoffs.

Chicago did in a big way for the next 28 seasons—second longest continuous playoff streak in the NHL.

GM Tommy Ivan picked up goalie Tony Esposito who had played a few games with Montreal after starring in college at Michigan Tech. Jim Wiste and Cliff Koroll starred for Denver University and had played the year before with the Hawk farm team in Dallas.

Keith Magnuson had co-captained Denver who won the NCAA championship over Ken Dryden's Cornell team, which gave the Hawks four U.S. college grad players on the team— a first for an NHL team.

The chemistry with veterans Mikita, Bobby and Dennis Hull, Pit Martin, Pappin, Stapleton, Nesterenko, Jarrett and the return of Lou Angotti clicked.

The season started off poorly with the Hawks winless in six games although they earned a 1-1 tie in the sixth game against New York on Koroll's first NHL goal.

Esposito made his presence felt in the seventh game which was his first appearance in Montreal against his former team on October 25, 1969. "Tony O" racked up his first shutout as a Hawk 5-0 over the Canadiens.

He went on to register 14 more to set a modern-day record of 15 in one season and win Rookie of the Year honors, the Vezina Trophy and was named first-team All-Star!

Five Empty-Net Goals and First Place

Chicago earned first place in the last game of the season April 5, 1970, in what was described as one of the strangest games ever at the Stadium. The Hawks needed a win to tie Boston, but would get the edge because of more wins. They were facing Montreal which needed a win or tie to get into the playoffs or they would be out for the first time in 22 years.

Montreal took an early lead and learned that the Rangers had already won their game which meant that unless they won, tied or scored at least five goals, they would be out.

Chicago rallied and took a 5-2 lead. In desperation with about 12 minutes left in regulation, Montreal pulled its goalie to try to get three more goals. Chicago took advantage to score five empty goals and clinch first place in the 10-2 win.

In the playoffs, the Hawks swept Detroit four straight by 4-2 scores to face Boston. The Bruins were paced by Bobby Orr who led the league in scoring with 120 points and Phil Esposito who had 43 goals and 99 points. The Bruins had too much scoring and swept Chicago four straight en route to their first Stanley Cup in 30 years with a four-game sweep of St. Louis.

1971 Playoffs: High...and Very Low

Besides my public address duties, I joined Lloyd Pettit in doing the color during the playoffs which necessitated a backup for the games at the stadium.

In the opening round, Chicago swept Philadelphia in

four games. Next came the Rangers in what I feel was the most exciting seven-game playoff series I ever witnessed. There were three overtime games and both teams played great hockey. I feel that even though the Hawks prevailed and moved into the finals against Montreal, the Rangers' series caused emotional and physical drain.

New York won the first game in Chicago on an overtime goal by Pete Stemkowski. The Hawks took the next, a 3-0 shutout by Tony Esposito. Back to Madison Square Garden, the Rangers came out on top 4-1, but the Hawks evened things with a 7-1 rout heading back to the Stadium.

The contest was tied 2-2 going into overtime. With a face off in the New York zone, Pit Martin got the draw back to Bobby Hull who fired in the game winner. The sixth game was a classic that went into the third overtime when Stemkowski won it to tie the series with the deciding game back in Chicago. The Hawks came out with a 4-2 triumph and the right to meet Montreal in the finals.

A lot has been written about that seven-game series and every Hawk player on that team I have talked to says they still think about it. The Hawks had home ice and the teams each split the first four games. Tony Esposito shut out Montreal 2-0 in Game 5 as the teams headed back to Montreal for Game 6. The Hawks built up a 2-0 lead going into the third period, but the Canadiens rallied to win 4-3 and tie the series.

The Hawks took a 2-0 lead in Game 7 in the second period. Cliff Koroll and Chico Maki had a two-man breakaway on goalie Ken Dryden but missed the net. Then Bobby Hull hit the crossbar.

It was a hot, muggy night May 18 in a jam-packed Stadium when Jacques LeMaire fired a shot from center ice that Esposito didn't pick up to cut the lead to 2-1. Just before the end of the second period, the reliable Eric Nesterenko lost the puck along the boards and Montreal's Henri Richard tied the game at 2-all. Early in the third period, Keith Magnuson was heading to the bench when the puck popped loose in center ice, as the speedy Richard had jumped over the boards to score on a breakaway to give the Canadiens the Cup. Jim Pappin had almost tied it in the final seconds and raised his arms signaling a goal, but Dryden made the save!

The Decade of the '70s

With the World Hockey Association coming and the NHL expanding, there was a dilution of the talent pool, but the Hawks were still a very talented team.

For the decade, Chicago finished first seven times, second once and third twice. More teams, more players, more difficult name pronunciations by the public address announcers. I know when I got the opportunity to go on the road and listen to my counterparts at different arenas, it was interesting.

While working at the Stadium before the games, I always made a point of talking to the radio-TV announcers to get their take or if the visitors' public relation director was available I would ask him. Sometimes I would get two or three different versions of the same name. When players were traded to the Hawks, it would take a game or two before I would be informed which way is right or wrong.

The east coast PA announcers had their way of saying

things. I remember in Boston when the announcer kept calling No. 16 Chico Maki (Mac-ee), Chico May-kee.

Potato or Pat-Tad-o?

Of course being human, we all make mistakes, however when you have a full stadium of some 17,000 fans hearing what you say, there's no place to hide your voice. Sometimes my tongue would get caught between my teeth in announcing. Then, some players would change how they wanted their names announced whether it was their last name or nickname.

I mentioned earlier that Bill Hay never wanted to be announced as Red. One of the players obtained with the big trade with Boston, Gilles Marotte, told me he would prefer to have me announce his name as "Gil."

I informed my backup PA guy, John Hogan, who worked at WGN, about his wishes. John told me when Lloyd Pettit (Hawks' play-by-play icon) announces as Gil, he will.

My favorite Hawk player's name to announce in the early '70s was goalie Gerry Desjardins. I asked him how would he like his name announced, Day-jarden, Duh-jarden, Day-jardeen or what? Gerry told me, "Whatever you like."

Baloney!

One player I remember kept changing his pronunciation. Dave Balon started his NHL career with the New York Rangers in 1959. He played 14 seasons in the league with New York, Montreal, Minnesota and Vancouver. When he was with the

Rangers, he went by Bahl-on. His first year in Montreal, it was Bay-lone, but the next year he was Buh-lone. After that I felt like calling him baloney!

The Russians are Coming!

In 1972, the NHL sanctioned a preseason series with the Canadian NHL stars and a Soviet National team. The Canadians, without WHA players such as Bobby Hull, prevailed in the eight game series, 4-3-1.

In January 1976, several Russian teams played exhibition games against NHL teams. The Stadium was the site on January 7, and the Soviets won 4-2. Even though my mother was born in Russia (she left when she was two), the only Russian I knew was vodka, caviar and borscht! I know I got most of their first names pronounced right: "Igor, Ivan, Boris, Alexi and John." All I remember about their last names were that they either ended in "nov" or "ski."

Changes in the '80s

New conference lineups, the mandatory wearing of helmets, number of players dressed, the merger of four WHA teams and a five-minute sudden death overtime all came about in the '80s.

All new players coming into the NHL had to wear helmets. Doug Wilson was one of the last Hawks to play without a helmet. Craig MacTavish, who played for 17 seasons, was the last player to not wear a helmet when he retired in 1997.

In the 10 years, the Hawks finished first on four occasions in the Smythe, then Norris Division with two seconds, two thirds and two fourths. Chicago went to the division and conference finals five times.

New Heights and Lows in the '90s

The Hawks started out the '90s strong, finishing first twice and second once, going to the conference finals in 1990 and the Stanley Cup finals in 1992.

The old Chicago Stadium closed in April 1994 and the new United Center hosted its first game January 25, 1995, because of the late start of the season due to the labor dispute.

The 1998 season saw the Hawks' 28 consecutive playoff appearances end, the second-longest streak in NHL history.

Many Milestones Reached

The Hawks hosted their fourth NHL All-Star game on January 19, 1991, days after the Persian Gulf War. A sell out crowd and a stiring rendition of the national anthem was a thrilling patriotic display.

A month later, Michel Goulet earned his 1,000th

Michel Goulet

NHL point and a year later, he registered his 500th career goal.

In the nets, Eddie Belfour broke Tony Esposito's record for wins with 43 in 1990-91, took the Vezina Trophy for goalies plus Rookie of the Year honors. He won the Vezina again in '93 and All-Star honors with a 41 victory performance to become the fifth goalie to record more than one 40-win season.

Jeremy Roenick became the third Hawk in history to get 50 goals in a season with 53 in 1991-92 and 50 the following season.

Steve Larmer scored his 400th Hawk career goal in January 1993.

Names Get Tougher

The heavier influx of European players made announcing their names more difficult, but at least the league started to provide a pronunciation guide.

It seemed that I couldn't go a game without mis-pronouncing Sergei Krivokrasov, who played in Chicago from 1992-1998, at least once.

Improved Sound

There's no doubt that nothing will ever replace the feeling that the Chicago Stadium had for hockey fans. Everyone was much closer to the action. I know I miss it even though the United Center is a modern state-of-the-art facility. There's one thing better for the fans in the UC: the sound system and the scoreboard. The sound system in the stadium had a lot of blind spots, and if you were in the upper mezzaine past row S, you couldn't hear or see the scoreboard.

One Minute Remaining in the Period

I guess imitation is the highest form of flattery.

In the United Center, sometimes in the old Stadium, when I would get ready to announce the final minute of each period, fans would yell out to me, "How much time is there left, Harvey?"

Despite what some fans think, there are even a few NHL rules for public address announcers. Starting lineups on penalties, visitors always are announced first. Goals and assists are announced twice. When the red goal light goes on and the play is under review or disallowed, the referee shall provide the information to be announced. Changing of goal credits. After a goal is scored, the referee tells the game time keeper to inform the official scorer who in his opinion scored.

However, the official scorer has the final decision on who to award the goal to. Now with video replay, the scorer has an opportunity to review the play between periods to make changes. Naturally, more honest players can inform the scorer if any "injustices" are done.

Visiting Officials Before the Game

There is a sign on the official's door that no one is permitted to enter without authorization and in the United Center, and there is a security guard. In the stadium, their dressing room was down the hall from the Hawks' locker room.

I can't remember the year I started going into their room before the game. The Hawk public relations office would put out a lineup sheet with the officials to the media before each home game. Sometimes an official is sick, injured or delayed by weather.

One time, one of the linesman got switched. It happened to be Bob Luther, who lived in St. Louis. I announced the name on the sheet and Luther's wife was listening on the radio. She didn't hear her husband's name announced and "wondered" where he was. The next time Bob came to the Stadium, he informed me of my error. In those days, the officials wore numbers without names, later they had names on their shirts, and now they are back to numbers.

Lost Referee Shirts?

The officials usually stayed at a hotel near O'Hare Airport and then used to battle traffic to the stadium. In fact, even now, they mostly stay out there. The current director of officiating is Andy VanHellemond.

I remember one game, Andy left his referee shirt in his hotel room by the airport and had to send a messenger to get his shirt.

Meanwhile, he had to borrow a shirt from the Blackhawks which was too small and had no name or number. Everytime Andy would come back to work in Chicago, I would ask him, "Are you to wear a shirt with your name or number?" Andy would just smile at me.

"Remember the Roar"

There's hasn't been a person yet that ever attended a Blackhawk game that I talked to that hasn't raved about the grand old Chicago Stadium. I was very lucky to have been the Stadium announcer for 33 of its 65-year history.

Regardless of whether it's been a player, coach or spectator, it's a deep feeling that's hard to describe.

The noise and the closeness to the action was great, whether it was the washrooms, no water fountains for many years, the balcony overhang of the back rows of the mezzanine, the old stadium clock or more.

Players told me of the chill they felt as they climbed the stairs from the locker room to the ice to hear the crowd roar and the song, "Here Come the Hawks."

It's ironic that the largest "official" announced crowd at the stadium was 20,960 in the playoffs against Minnesota on April 10, 1982 when the Hawks lost 7-1, but won the series and went on to the conference finals. For many years, the official seating capacity was 16,666, but seats were added to make it 17,317 without standing-room crowds. Before that, the largest crowd came on February 9, 1947 against Boston when rookie goalie Emile "the Cat" Francis made his NHL debut with a 6-4 victory.

I know when I read the closing speech at the last game I felt a great deal of emotion. I didn't write it and I don't know who did, but it really hit a "hat trick" of feelings about that great Chicago Stadium!

Last Game at Chicago Stadium— April 14,1994 Read by Public Address Announcer Harvey Wittenberg Remember the Roar: Final Speech

"Ladies and gentlemen, may I have your attention for one last message. This is a message from the Chicago Blackhawks to you, the Chicago Blackhawk fans.

"For 65 years here at the Chicago Stadium, ordinary, hard-working people known as the Blackhawk fans have come together to create an extraordinary atmosphere.

"You have devoted your emotions to the Blackhawks and have become an important part of the team. Your loud and affectionate praise have given us an advantage that is unmatched in professional sports play. You have affected the lives and lifted the performances of every hockey player ever to skate on the Stadium ice. We look upon you as ideal fans: hard-working, devoted assets. And we thank you for this.

"Here in the Chicago Stadium, performance is not just on the ice, the performance is everywhere: in the hallways, in the organ loft, the banners throughout the mezzanine and the balconies. Together we have created something exceptional. The Chicago Stadium experience has been truly special.

"As you leave tonight, we ask that you:

Remember the great lady known as the Chicago Stadium—

Remember how it was built to happen—

Remember the championship banners swaying gently

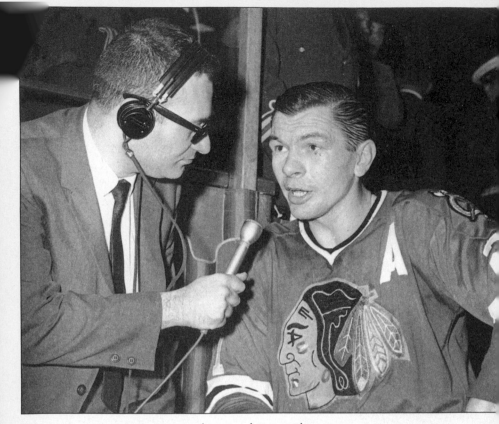

Harvey Wittenberg and Stan Mikita. Photo courtesy of Louie Okun

in the rafters—

Remember the people you sat next to 10 years ago that are your friends today—

Remember the organ loft and the press box and your favorite seat—

Remember the stairs leading all the way up to the second balcony—

Remember your favorite great players whether they are Bobby Hull, Jeremy Roenick, Tony Esposito, Eddie Belfour, Stan Mikita, Denis Savard, Keith Magnuson and Chris Chelios—

Remember the feeling you have right now!

"On behalf of the Chicago Blackhawks, thank you for making all of this possible and . . .

REMEMBER THE ROAR!"

Captain—Not Serious!

Already on his way to be one of the best Hawk players in team history, it is hard to realize that Jonathan Toews's potential keeps growing at a player in his twenties. His accomplishments already include a Stanley Cup, Conn Smythe Trophy as MVP of the playoffs, contender for the Hart Trophy as the NHL's MVP, just to mention a few. There is one thing he made clear to me—"Call me anything—but NOT Captain Serious!"

Jonathan reminds me of the type player that fits the mold of Chris Chelios and Keith Magnuson. Giving 100% all of the time is not enough and he wants to lead by example. He told me he is constantly trying to improve and never wants to lose. He realizes that after winning the Cup in 2010 that you have to keep raising the bar.

Being the overall third selection in the 2006 NHL draft, Jonathan is one of three Hawks born in Winnipeg, along with Duncan Keith and Patrick Sharp. Although the NHL doesn't keep every record, Jonathan scored his first NHL goal on his first shot on goal against San Jose at the United Center on October 10, 2007. Also he wound up that season as the top rookie goal scorer (24) and finished behind teammate Patrick Kane in Calder Trophy voting. With only seven other teammates on the 2011-12 roster from the 2010 Cup squad, Jonathan told me that a new chemistry is building and he's glad that Chicago is his home.

Toews-Kane Versus Mikita-Hull

Some may want to draw similarities between the Toews/ Kane duo to the Hawk heroes of the '60s—Stan Mikita and Bobby Hull. While Stan and Bobby seldom played on the same line except in power play situations, Toews and Kane have been together many times during their current Chicago careers. Usually, the coach feels that most times they can be more effective on different lines to drive their opponents crazy. They both share the same passion for winning and playing for the Hawks which was the main reason they both agreed to long term contracts to stay in Chicago instead of trying to hold out for much more money when their rookie contracts ended.

Kane displays the more "flashy" offensive moves, but has improved his defensive game while Toews provides a more overall steady performance on both ends of the ice in addition to being one of top faceoff centers. It's exciting to realize they are still in the early stages of their careers.

Toews Comparisons

I've spoke to a dozen former players, coaches, scouts, and broadcasters asking who they would compare Toews to, and one answer comes back—at his current age he is far ahead of most great players at this stage in his career. Names like Steve Yzerman, Joe Sakic, and Bryan Trottier have been mentioned among great forwards plus having the focus game in and game out with the likes of Chris Chelios and Keith Magnuson. Hopefully he will continue his career where he already has become the second youngest team captain to win a Stanley Cup.

Newest Norris Trophy Winner

Duncan Keith became the fourth Hawk to win the NHL's trophy as the NHL's best defenseman in 2010. A tireless skater, Duncan has been among the league's leaders in ice time. He told me winning the Norris along with the Stanley Cup is a great feeling to be honored along with the likes of Chris Chelios, Bobby Orr, and Nicklas Lidstrom. He along with Brent Seabrook have been with the Hawks the longest on their 2011-12 roster.

Just last year in wanting to give more back to the families in Chicagoland, Duncan and his wife, Kelly-Rae, established a new charity aimed at alleviating financial and emotional burdens suffering from medical crisis. With a long-term contract, Duncan wants to bring the cup back to Chicago fans again and feels the city's fans are great to play for and wants to reward them even more.

Hawk Cup Veterns Under 30

It may be hard to believe that the two "oldest" Hawk players from the 2010 Cup team are both under 30, but both Brent Seabrook and Duncan Keith share that distinction! Both joined the Hawks in the 2005-06 campaign with Seabrook being a first round draft pick in 2003 and Keith a second rounder in 2002.

The old man in terms of Hawk time is Patrick Sharp who came via a trade with Philadelphia in December 2005.

"Seabs" told me he never expected to see such a fast change in team chemistry from when he started with the Hawks up to winning the cup in 2010. When teaming up with Keith, the defensive pair was considered among the best in the NHL. Reflecting on the comeback victory in the first round overtime in Game 5 against Nashville, "We were lucky but I feel that it helped giving us a positive feeling that we could go all the way!"

Three Times Proved to be the Charm

Marian Hossa became the first NHL player to play in three straight Stanley Cup finals with three different teams, and fortunately the third time was the lucky charm as he was part of the 2010 Chicago cup winners. After being with Pittsburgh in 2008 and Detroit in 2009, the world class veteran agreed to a long term deal with the Hawks. "I love Chicago. It has a great atmosphere and winning the cup for the fans makes it even more special."

"I was worried that in that fifth game against Nashville that my penalty late in the third period would cost my team the game, and I was fortunate to score the winner after coming out of the penalty box to help us on the way to the Cup!"

Sharp Move

Patrick Sharp feels that the 2005 trade from the Flyers to the Blackhawks gave him the opportunity to show what he could do after he found it tough to break into the NHL with Philadelphia. Now with a long term contract and being a new father in 2011, "Sharpie" has consistently gotten better each season with the Hawks. "Being part of the new winning tradition in Chicago, it has been a life changer for me which makes it a lot of fun coming to play." Besides playing in the 2009 Winter Classic at Wrigley Field, Sharp won MVP honors in the 2011 All Star game.

Foley Dream Comes True

Fan favorite broadcaster, Pat Foley, realized a dream come true when he returned to the Chicago TV booth to do the play by play for the Blackhawks. The area native aired the Hawks for 25 seasons before a two year hiatus. "When President John McDonough called me and asked me to return, at first I didn't believe it. I didn't expect it and while I always loved doing the Hawks, I really had to pinch myself a few times to make sure I wasn't dreaming. Now, I couldn't be happier besides working with Eddie Olczyk."

Winning Coach

Replacing one of the Hawk's fan favorites, Denis Savard, early in the 2008 season, Joel Quennville became the 37th coach in Chicago history amid some controversy. However, with a squad that was one of the youngest in the NHL, the veteran coach proved to be the right tonic in leading the Hawks to their first Stanley Cup in 49 seasons and fourth overall. Joel is only one of three men who have played and coached in more than 800 NHL games, and has more than 600 victories as a head coach.

Marc Bergevin, now assistant Hawk GM, played with, against, was coached by, and served as an assistant to Joel during their long association. It was their relationship that led Joel to Chicago. After the 2007-08 campaign in Colorado, Joel planned to take some time off to spend with his family. Marc contacted him to join the Hawks as a pro scout to start the 2008-09 season, but Joel wound up being named head coach on October 16th.

Core Strength

"Because of the salary cap after we won the Cup, we were forced to make many changes, but I feel we have a solid nucleus with a lot of promising youngsters as we move forward." Looking back on the 2010 champs, Joel said, "We got lucky in some craziest situations. Probably our defining moment was Patrick Kane's shorthanded goal in the closing seconds to tie Game 5 against Nashville in the opening round which gave us added confidence as we moved through the playoffs."

Bergevin Pranks

While playing for Joel for St. Louis in the 1999 playoffs, Bergevin, did one that Joel remembered. "It was the seventh and deciding game in Phoenix in the opening round. Marc

Coach Joel Quennville lifting the Stanley Cup after the 4-3 overtime win in Philadelphia on June 9, 2010.

wasn't playing, but when the team bus pulled up to the arena, Marc stood outside the bus with sign saying "GO BLUES!" The Blues in fact prevailed 1-0 in overtime!

United Center Debut

The lack of a new player agreement resulted in a shortened season in 1994-95. So the 48 game schedule didn't start until January 20, 1995. The Hawks played their first game at the new United Center on January 25th. Joe Murphy had the first Hawk goal scored at the UC in a 5-1 victory over Edmonton.

Murphy Trade Deal

Murphy, a colorful character in his four Hawk seasons, told Hawk Coach Darryl Sutter to pick up free agent center Bernie Nicholls who was not resigned by New Jersey during the lockout. In fact Murphy bragged that if they made the deal, he would score at least 30 goals. Darryl told Joe, "We don't need another flake on the team." Darryl must have been kidding because the Hawks did pick up Nicholls the next year and led the team in points (51) in the 48 game schedule. Also, Bernie did have two four-goal games in his brief two years with the Hawks.

On the other hand, Murphy did bag 31 goals in 1993-94, but only scored 23 and 22 while playing with Nicholls. While Murphy played for seven different NHL teams in 15 seasons and did have the distinction of being the first collegiate player ever to be drafted first overall when picked by Detroit in 1986 after starring for Michigan State.

Unusual Hawk Trivia

Darren Pang holds the Hawk record for most points by a Hawk goalie with six assists in 1987-88 which was only one point less than defensemen Marc Bergevin and Dave Manson. Steve Dubinsky holds the team record for wearing the most different numbered jerseys in his eight seasons with the Hawks.

Steve had to buy his own program to see what he was wearing each year as he donned #42, 29, 32, 22, 14,and 16.

Rocky Wirtz Era—Positive Path

Winning a Stanley Cup, having a long waiting list for season tickets and having more than 150 consecutive sellouts in leading the NHL in attendance might lead one to think that you can rest on your laurels—"NO" is the answer I got from Blackhawk owner Rocky Wirtz.

"We want to keep getting better and continue to show our fans that we listen to their concerns. When I took over, we didn't have many good relationships with a lot people." One of early moves was to lure John McDonough away from the Cubs to bring on board as team president. McDonough not only brought a new philosophy to the Blackhawks, but made a number of changes in attitude to embrace former players like Bobby Hull, Stan Mikita, Denis Savard, and Tony Esposito.

April Fool's Delight

It was not a prank when Rocky and McDonough announced that for the first time that all Hawk home games would be shown on TV starting in the 2008-09 season. That was just a continuing flow of positive news that endeared Rocky to Hawk fans. While most owners prefer to sit in sky-boxes, Rocky has opted to sit in the stands among the fans.

Lottery Winner—Compares to Denis Savard

After landing North Dakota freshman Jonathan Toews, third overall in the 2006 draft, the Hawks were scheduled to get the fifth overall pick in 2007. However, lady luck intervened when the pre-draft lottery was held and with odds of 15-1 against moving up, the Hawks grabbed the number one spot ahead of Philadelphia, Phoenix, Los Angeles, and Washington. Patrick Kane, an 18 year old from Buffalo, was the choice which has proved to be the most exciting Hawk offensive player in recent years.

Denis Savard was went to the Hawks in 1980 as the third overall selection as the result of a trade with the Quebec Nordiques, who came over from the World Hockey Association, allowing Chicago to move up in the draft from the 15th spot. The Hawks held the NHL rights to Nordiques star right wing Real Cloutier, who Chicago had made their first round pick in 1976. Quebec surrendered the third overall pick in the draft so they could keep Cloutier instead of losing him to the Hawks as part of the merger agreement between the leagues.

Kane—More than Able!

The Buffalo native who grew up idolizing the likes of Pat LaFontaine (468 goals) and Alexander Mogilny (473 goals) made an immediate impact in 2007-08 by winning top rookie honors with the Calder Trophy while leading the team in points (72). He became the eighth Hawk to capture that award—the first since 1991 when goalie Ed Belfour was honored.

Dream Goal

Kane told me growing up that dreaming of scoring a goal to win the Stanley Cup is something, but actually accomplishing it is a different story. "It was unbelievable. I knew it was in and I guess I went a little wild throwing my gloves and stick in the air and skating to the other end trying to sell the celebration to my teammates."

Many Flyer players and fans on June 9, 2010 may still be stunned at that overtime goal. Of course, not to be overlooked was his shorthanded goal with 13.6 seconds in Game 5 with Nashville in the opening playoff round to send into overtime leading to Marian Hossa's winner, enabling the Hawks to eventually move on their way to their first Cup in 49 years.

Youngest Hawk GM Ever

Coming from a rich tradition of hockey whose father (Scotty) is the winningest coach in NHL history, Stan Bowman became the ninth Hawk General Manager, and the youngest in history. With almost a dozen years with the Hawks while presiding over the Stanley Cup win at the age of 36, Stan joined the staff in 2001 as a special assistant to the GM and was promoted to VP/GM in September 2010.

GM Role Changes

Before the days of the hard salary caps, NHL general managers mainly were more involved with player evaluations, and coaching decisions to go with salary negotiations. Stan told me, "Today I would define my position of being more of a business manager...There are more challenges today to balance things while dealing with the present and constantly planning for the future. After winning the Cup, I knew we had to make a lot of very tough decisions to keep the core of our team together which I feel we have achieved. I feel fortunate that with the current atmosphere and the backing of Rocky Wirtz and John McDonough, players like Toews, Kane, Keith, Seabrook, Hossa, and Sharp to mention a few have agreed to long term deals because they want to play for Chicago."

Draft Deal Stockpiles

While being forced to make trades due the salary cap, Bowman with the aid of his staff have managed to build up a number of promising players which should continue to make the Hawks a strong contender for years.

Special Thoughts

Commenting on that fateful Game 5 against Nashville in the Cup year, "It was an unbelievable comeback, but one

I always remained optimistic." Also, Stan felt in 2011 when after down three games in the opening round against Vancouver and fighting back to tie Game 7 on Toews's late goal, "We were only one shot away from moving on in overtime."

Fatherly Advice

Growing up in Montreal while his father, Scotty, was coaching the Canadiens, Stan had an early taste of hockey tradition. Scotty joined the Hawks as a Senior Advisor in July, 2008 which became just the 10th father-son GM combo in NHL annals besides being just the fourth pair to have their names on the Stanley Cup.

I asked Stan what was the best piece of advice that his father gave him since he took over as Hawk GM and he told me "To win consistently, you have to get the best out of your best players!"

New Path—New President

When Rocky Wirtz named John McDonough Blackhawk President in November 2007, a new positive chapter began and took a bigger jump with the Stanley Cup in June 2010. In preparation for the city celebration on June 10th, John was asked how was he going to handle the festivities, "I don't know. Being with the Cubs for a long time (24 years), I never had to deal with anything like it!"

Looking Forward

When John was introduced as the new team president, one of the first questions asked was what was his plan to get Blackhawk fans back? "Start winning is the first step and look ahead, not back." While I have listed a number achievements earlier that has come about from John's leadership, I think that developing a positive attitude toward the fans with hiring the right people to carry out those plans has translated into success.

"Rocky Wirtz has allowed me to do what was needed even made it came to making tough decisions that weren't always done in the past. Reaching out to bring back Mikita and Hull, televising home games, bringing back Pat Foley plus honoring former players like Chris Chelios, Jeremy Roenick, and Ed Belfour in addition to saluting the 1961 Cup team. Also, I was fortunate in being able, with a lot of help, in securing the Winter Classic at Wrigley Field on January 1, 2009."

Building Teamwork

John used his Cubs experience in bringing on board a number of key personnel that he worked with like Senior VP of Business Operations, Jay Blunt, who spent 22 years with the baseball club. Needless to say, the two sports are a lot different in preparation. Jay told me that with the Cubs he would stop in the locker room before a game to talk with the players. Early on with the Hawks, he decided to do the same before the players took the ice for the pregame warm-ups. "Let's say with their game focus on, I was given an icy stare and shown the door!"

Stan Mikita and Bobby Hull viewing the HD Video scoreboard from a United Center suite that was showing their newly unveiled statues outside the UC.

October 22, 2011—Mikita/Hull Statues

Another Hawk tribute to honor two of the team's greatest players, Stan Mikita and Bobby Hull, came with the unveiling of the statues, side by side, on the northeast side of the United Center. The likeness of the two Hall of Famers came from the works of Julie Rotblatt Amrany and Omri Amrany who also created the Michael Jordan statue. Both Mikita and Hull were deeply touched and humbled by the event and the words of Rocky Wirtz about the Hawk icons.

Anthem History

The Blackhawks have a rich tradition in the singing of our National Anthem going back to the late 1940s when the team had soloists from Chicago's Lyric Opera. During the 1980s playoffs against Edmonton, fans began cheering and applauding while Wayne Messmer was singing. Some from other cities felt this might be disrespectful, but I like most feel it is honoring our country. Most in attendance at the Stadium on January 19, 1991 shortly after the outbreak of the Persian Gulf War, as the Hawks hosted the NHL All Star game , were overwhelmed with emotion as fans waved the flag and cheered. Current soloist Jim Cornelison evokes the same emotion as he sings the anthem at home games, and was at one of his finest moments at the Wrigley Field Winter Classic against the Red Wings.

Superstitious "13"

John Wiedeman, current radio by play by play voice of the Hawks, , once confided to his color analyst and former Hawk player, Troy Murray about his phobia regarding the number 13. Troy jumped at a chance to kid his radio partner when the Tampa Bay Lightning came to the United Center on December 13, 2009. John told me that Troy had plastered the radio booth with the number which kind of freaked him out during the broadcast. Fortunately it didn't affect him or the team as they blanked the Lightning 4-0.

13th Pick in 1972

The Hawks had the 13th draft pick in 1972 and came up with defenseman Phil Russell, who made the team at the age of 20 in their first season without Bobby Hull. The 6'2" 200 pounder made an instant impression with 156 penalty minutes, ending Keith Magnuson's three year run leading that category.

Fiery Tempers From Fiery Competitors

There's probably not one player who hates to lose any game, but the Hawks had two who always made no bones about expressing it more than Chris Chelios or Ed Belfour. In 1991 with Mike Keenan as coach and Belfour in his rookie year, Mike would show video between periods and after the game. In one of his rare off nights on his way to rookie honors Ed was very upset and when Mike left the locker room— wham, bam there was a broken goalie stick and a smashed $6,000 video camera.

Scotty Bowman has called Chelios one of most competitive players he ever coached. So there isn't any surprise one night when Keenan benched him in the third period of a game in 1991. Right after the game, Cheli tore down to the locker room and trashed Keenan's office.

Hawks Single Game Goal Record

When you think of top Hawk goal scorers, most would name Bobby Hull, Stan Mikita, Denis Savard, Steve Larmer, or Jeremy Roenick. However, the single game mark of five goals belongs to Grant Mulvey. "Granny" scored five against St. Louis at the Stadium on February 3, 1982. He lit the lamp four times in the opening period and added a fifth in the third to go along with two assists, tying a team mark set 39 years earlier by Max Bentley.

Grant told me that he didn't feel well that day and in the pregame skate fell twice in addition to breaking his stick. "On my first shift, my shot went in off the shaft of the goalie's stick, the next two were rebounds, then off a faceoff with the other coming from assists from Savard and Terry Ruskowski. I might had a chance for another, but I got into a fight and sat out seven minutes in the penalty box in the second period.

Four Goals for & Against—Pit Martin

Pit Martin, who drowned in a freak accident a few years ago, is the only NHL player I know who scored four goals in a game for and against the Hawks. In January 1966, Pit was playing for Boston after being traded from Detroit. The Hawks were playing back to back games with Stan Mikita being sidelined. They beat Montreal 4-2 the night before and had called up minor league scorer, Art Stratton from their Buffalo AHL team. However, the speedy Martin skated circles around

Stratton with four goals in a 5-3 Bruin win. Three years later on March 30, 1969 in a Hawk uniform, Pit scored four goals against Detroit, the team that originally drafted him, in a 9-5 victory at the Stadium. Hawk defenseman Pat Stapleton set a Chicago with six assists in that game.

First Hawk Selke Winner— Troy Murray

Troy Murray, besides being color analyst for more than a dozen seasons, was the first Hawk to win the Selke Trophy in 1986 as the NHL's best defensive forward. Dirk Graham won it in 1991. Troy had a banner year with 45 goals and 54 assists. He was a third round pick in 1980 after playing for North Dakota, the college Jonathan Toews, Ed Belfour, and John Marks all attended.

One of the most important goals in Troy's career came on the season finale at the Stadium on April 2, 1989 against Toronto. The NHL resumed overtime games in 1983-84 after a 41 year lapse. The Hawks needed a victory to beat out the Maple Leafs for the last playoff spot. Troy delivered the game winner in overtime. The Hawks went on to the conference finals before bowing to Calgary—the eventual Cup Champion.

Keenan's Dog House

It was Troy's tenth season with the Hawks in 1991 when, like several players, he got into Mike Keenan's doghouse. The fiery coach had cut Troy's ice time and the team was having an "off night" in Toronto. In fact, Troy hadn't seen any action the entire game. So with less than three minutes to play, he loosened the laces on his skates. Naturally, Iron Mike yelled to him to get on the ice. Troy immediately fell, much to his chagrin. Troy was traded to Winnipeg at the end of the season, but returned to Hawks in 1992-93 when Darryl Sutter was coaching.

Dumb Bell Skates

Coaches have different ways of informing players that were not playing the night of a game. Billy Reay would tell the trainer not to take that individual's skates out of their bags when they came to the arena. That was the practice for many. However, Hawk defenseman Bryan Marchment took exception one night when Coach Darryl Sutter scratched him in 1992. Marchment picked up a dumbbell and threw it against the wall. After that, Sutter had the trainer put a dumbbell in front of the locker when a player was scratched.

Open Goal—A "Rocky" Start = Success!

It took seven seasons after Blackhawk owners Arthur Wirtz and Jim Norris hired Tommy Ivan away from Detroit to become general manager and bring the Stanley Cup back to Chicago after a 23 year drought in 1961. On the other hand, under the leadership of W. "Rocky" Wirtz, who took over on October 5, 2007 , the elusive Stanley Cup ended a 49 year absence on June 9, 2010 with an overtime win in Philadelphia. One second really separated victory from possible defeat in 2010 and that's really how close and difficult it is to win or even repeat as a champion in the days of the NHL salary cap. Marian Hossa's dramatic goal against Nashville at 4:07 of overtime came after getting out of the penalty box after Patrick Kane tied the game on a shorthander with less than 14 seconds remaining in regulation time. The victory gave the Hawks a 3-2 series edge in the best of seven. Ironically on June 9th, Patrick Kane's cup winning goal came a second earlier (4:06) in overtime, and the mystery of where the puck went after going past goalie Michael Leighton still hasn't been solved.

Complete Turnaround for Team and Fans

The Rocky Wirtz Era in a period of a few seasons has produced almost too many great things for the fans and players to even list, but I will give it a shot. It has to start with the hiring of John McDonough as President in November 2007. John, a long time Blackhawk fan, had been with the Cubs for 24 years. Less than a month into the job, John invited fan favorites Stan Mikita and Bobby Hull to rejoin the Hawks

Blackhawk Hall of Fame Ambassadores in the team locker room.
(L-R)} Denis Savard (18), Stan Mitika (21), Tony Esposito (35),
and Bobby Hull (9).

as team ambassadors and later added Hall of Famers Tony
Esposito and Denis Savard.

Not an April Fool's Joke!

For the 1st time in Blackhawk history, Rocky Wirtz and
John McDonough announced on April 1, 2008 that starting

next season all games home and road would be televised much to the delight of all Chicago fans.

Hawk Voice—Pat Foley Returns!

After two year hiatus, McDonough announced in June 2008 that the Blackhawk voice for 25 seasons, Pat Foley, would return as the play by play voice on all TV games for the 2008-09 campaign.

Winter Classic Scheduled for Wriggley Field

Again through the efforts of Rocky and John, the NHL announced that the Blackhawks would host archrival and defending Cup Champs, Detroit, in a regular season battle outdoors at Wrigley Field on January 1,2009—only the second time that the outdoor classic would be held in the United States.

First NHL Fan Convention

McDonough, who had been instrumental in starting fan conventions while with the Cubs, saw almost 10,000 Hawk fans attend the first-ever such NHL event at the Hilton Chicago July 18-20, 2008 and has been selling out since with fans coming from all over North America to meet current and past players and coaches.

All Time Winning NHL Coach Joins Hawks

Scotty Bowman joined the Hawks as Senior Advisor of hockey operations on July 31, 2008 after being part of 11 Stanley Cup winners and the all time coach in NHL history with 1,244 regular season victories. He won his 12th Cup in 2009-10 with the Hawks.

First Ever Fan Festival

The Blackhawks hosted their 1st ever Training Camp festival on September 20, 2008 at the United Center.

Quenneville Hired as Coach

With one of the youngest teams in the NHL, the Hawks turned to veteran coach and player Joel Quennville on October 16, 2008 to become the team's 37th coach in their 85 year history.

Honoring the #3 Jersey

The Blackhawks honored two of their players that wore #3 by retiring their jerseys. Both were captains, Hall of Famer Pierre Pilote and the late Keith Magnuson.

Winter Classic January 1, 2009

Nearly 41,000 fans jammed Wrigley Field for the NHL Winter Classic to see the first-ever outdoor professional hockey game played in Chicago as the Red Wings edged the Hawks 6-4.

Return to the Playoffs

The Hawks returned to the playoffs for the first time since 2002 when they beat Nashville 3-1 on April 3, 2009 at the United Center on their way to setting a franchise attendance record and an NHL mark with an average of 21,783 fans per game.

Turnaround Team of the Year

Forbes.com stated on May 18, 2009 that the Blackhawks are "the Greatest Sports-Business Turnaround Ever."

Stan Bowman Named Youngest GM Ever

Stan Bowman, in his eighth season as assistant general manager, was named the ninth GM of the Hawks on July 14, 2009—the youngest in team history.

Stanley Cup 2010

Patrick Kane's overtime in Game 6 at Philadelphia on June 9, 2010, gave Chicago its fourth Stanley Cup and firstt since 1961.

Presidential Honor

The 2010 Stanley Cup Champions were honored at the White House on March 11, 2011.